THE LIGHT:
Fighting Physical and Spiritual Sexual Demons

When the Darkness is
A Family Member

Memoir of

Ellena M. Smith

ISBN: 9798342294126

DEDICATION

This book is dedicated to several people, each person played a pivotal role in my life story and was the influence for me to write this book.

First to Alysa, my firstborn. The first person to show me what real love felt like. My original road dog. As a young mother, I made so many mistakes with you that I can never take back. But regardless of all my shortcomings as a mother, you always saw the light in me. Even when we didn't understand each other. When you watched me go through relationship after relationship. The fights in my relationships, the suffering, all the moving around. Even when I made you become the head of the household and manage your siblings while I went out to work, I didn't allow you to be a child. Something I had despised my own mother for as a child, that she did to my older sisters, but now I was forced to do that which I saw as her flaw. You saw me as a thug, fighting people in the streets, and me as a loose cannon. We went through a period of not communicating so often, because of different worldly views. But now look at us. You are my everything and I thank you for being my Rock!

Symone, if Ride or Die had a picture, your face would be it. After Alysa left, you had to move up to the new position of head of the house, and you took your role seriously! During our Tastee Treatz days, you were my accountability partner. And the role you played with your baby sister during her sickness showed me every bit of greatness that you are. We stayed glued at the hip, I saw your hustle, hard work, and dedication to whatever it is you do. Always my feisty one, and if it wasn't done your way you weren't having no part in it! You always make me want to do and be better. I love that you gave me standards to live up to and because of you I always want to be the best version of myself. I don't want you to read this book, lol because I know you already know some of the things I've gone through in life, but I feel my harsh reality may be too much for you to bear. So, after this dedication put the book down. Pahaha! You gave me an amazing son-in-law and four of the most beautiful and perfect grandchildren any mother could ask for. Keep being the greatness you have always been, I love you with my whole heart!

Imani, I know you heard the stories of me being depressed throughout my pregnancy with you, there's also a little more to the story, but who needs all the details? All I know is that from the time I looked at you, I understood how perfect God is! You are and have always been a beam of light that exudes the presence of Love. You are Love in a whole person. You are gentle and kind and always my most maintenance-free child. You didn't cry as a baby or as a child. Everyone who looked into your face always saw pure innocence and you are and have always been exactly what I needed. Your hugs and your kisses were the sweetest thing a mother could receive when you were young. Again, you are now and then and always exactly what I need in life and I am so thankful to God for blessing me with your presence. You are my Love, and you are Love!

Zory, you are my spirit child and I am convinced our energy has lived several lives together. Funny when you entered our home, I had no idea what, or who you would end up being to me. It was rough beginnings because I thought you were just a bratty, smart-mouth teen lol. But once I learned who you are I discovered the strength, the fighter, the resilient warrior that you are. Coming into our world you have been exposed to this crazy energy that follows me. I'm not sure if we have energies that intertwined, but I know we've experienced some stuff together. I am more than ecstatic to be your bonus mom, and it's a title I don't take lightly. You taught me to love a child outside of my own, which matured me in ways that you don't even know. But just know this, I will always be there for you as if I gave birth to you myself. I love you to the end of the earth, and I am so happy that you and Alysa became friends, because of that friendship you became family!

Oh, Damany! You came here on fire! From the story of your birth and the confusion of your actual birthdate to the screaming and crying, the running and the jumping. The whippings and the scoldings. Putting SpaghettiOs up your nose, smearing food all over your head, or throwing eggs at people in restaurants! You were a whole character, but guess what? When I was pregnant with you, I said I just want a badass little boy, and man we have to be careful with what we ask for lol! But it's so crazy who you have become in the last few years. Yes, preteen we fought daily and I had to go hardcore on you. I'm happy I did because you are Perfect! During Easy Days you became my protector and I never felt so safe in my life than when you were by my side. You was not playing with them, crackheads. And I saw that you was not playing about yo mama! Today is your 19th birthday and I never imagined we would be so close. You know more about me than your sisters have ever known. You ask me questions and you don't let up until I give you an answer. Even when I tell you, you don't want to know, your response is oh yes, I want to know! You are the exact son I prayed to God for and I feel more than blessed to have you by my side. I know, as you grow and mature my time with you is limited, because soon you'll meet someone and a new woman will be in your life. But what I do know is that we have a strong bond that can never be broken. You have been the foundation that held me together and for that Bro, our Love is unmeasurable!

My sweet Alaia! My superhero! You entered the world with what most would see as struggles. But we know what it is, Strength Training and Character Building. Because of you, I went on my Spiritual journey. Because of you, I met God face to face. Because of you, I left every bit of the bad side of me behind, I had to become better because of YOU! Your strength is unmatched. Cancer came you kicked its butt. Diabetes came you kicked its butt. Unresponsive with cancer, pulled through in hours. Coma for 3 days with Diabetes. Pulled through like a champ! You have given me the worst scares of my life, but I put all my trust and faith in God and never panicked or worried because I know that you are Divinely Protected and there is a special covering over your life. You showed me that I am the Mother of Creation. Because you are a Divine Creation! You dance, you sing, you play, you laugh like no other. The world to you is a playground and you enjoy every moment of it. My Love Bug! The Cancer 69 in you makes you overly huggy, overly kissy, overly touchy. But it's exactly what I needed because before you I didn't like to be touched or hugged or kissed on too much. But you made me realize that's a Trauma Response that needed to be healed. The word Love can't even describe how I feel about you! My Lailai!

Bear with me, I'm almost done but my brother Ken. You have rode with me through this whole book. Because of you, this story has the adventure that it needs. We rolled the streets of LA, thugging! I know you always wanted to look out for me, but I was a force to be reckoned with and there was no controlling me. So, you always watched from the background. Thank you for always being more than you thought you were. I needed you throughout my life, and I love and thank you for that!

This book is also dedicated to all the mentors and friends who have come across my energy. Uncle Deese, you taught me the art of entrepreneurship. If there was a business venture to be looked into you was checking it out. My step-father Willie Hurd, you showed me what hard work looked like. You took care of my mother and us children as though we were your own. Thank you for loving me. Lawrence Ennis, you always knew my worth and supported me wholeheartedly. Thank you for every opportunity you've ever given me. Sparkle, for giving me a platform with the youth of Las Vegas, Summer Blast Day Camp, bringing life to Easy Days with your events and connections, and being a safe space for me. Love you sis! Chef Jeff and the Chef Jeff Project! You constantly told me my story was unique and riveting, and putting this book out would be just what somebody who may be going through something needs to read! Thank you for pushing me to finish this book, with your no-BS hardcore attitude to life! You are all such a blessing!

And lastly, this book is dedicated to the little child who lost their innocence to a monster that lives in their home or visits their home, or whose home they may visit. The little child who doesn't have a voice to speak up or out against predators. The child who hides their pain in silence, while it destroys them on the inside. To the teenager who has been destroyed by sexual violence. The teenager who constantly thinks of causing harm to themselves because no one sees or hears them. To the teenager that has destructive behaviors because of your pain, or the teenager that is closed off and silent, living in a world that feels distant or alien to their own woes and troubles. And to the unhealed adults, who navigated through this life in all their pain and all their misery, but all the while remaining strong, getting up every day, showing up for their families, for work, and relationships, knowing people don't and won't ever understand you! It's tough!

The hardest part of depression is pretending you're not depressed! As a black woman in America, I was always told that Black people don't get depressed. We just keep moving. Well, guess what? Black people get depressed and we keep moving because we have no choice, but every part of our existence in America is unhealthy. Black women are the most unprotected group of people on the planet. But we are the backbone of the world! I pray this book reaches the hands of someone who takes notice of odd behavior in a child and can ask them the right questions to expose their pain. Or someone who notices a teen who is depressed and can get them the help they need to turn their life around before they become an unhealed adult. Or to the hands of an unhealed adult who struggles with seeing their purpose in life. Someone who feels unmotivated to keep going. I pray they realize that everyone has a purpose and a reason to live and that every single thing that happens on this earth happens by design, whether good or bad. And your experiences are meant as a training tool and a lesson. Don't you ever give up! God is real and waiting at the finish line for us to cross over.

I Love You!

CONTENTS

THE LIGHT

El means THE or GOD. Lena means LIGHT. I named this book THE LIGHT because my name Ellena means THE LIGHT! Spending your entire life trying to figure out why you had to endure so much hardship is one part of the mission. Discovering the WHY and what to do with it is the next.

INTRODUCTION

Writing this book has been the hardest thing I have ever done in my life. Putting on paper the life that I lived was an internal battle. I didn't write this book with the intention of hurting anyone, or to ruffle any feathers. I wrote this book because it deals with subjects that are considered taboo. These are subjects that people don't want to talk about because it shouldn't even happen, but it does. This book may upset some people, but in life -in society- we become so fixated on protecting the reputation of individuals who are predators, that we forget there is a victim whose life has been ruined by the actions of such. As a victim, you rarely have a voice. You're quieted by fear! Fear of retaliation, fear of rejection, fear of accusations of false claims, fear of being called crazy, or fear of violence. So, you stay quiet and you suffer in silence.

For some reason, predators are usually people who are liked or loved by many. They are very clever at appearing to be the social butterfly, the life of the party, or the fun person to be around. The people on the outside never see the monster that these people really are. So, when the victim comes out and makes a claim of abuse, instantly everyone says "No way! Not him. Not her! He or She is such a good person! I would have never imagined that they would do such a thing!"

Being a victim is very daunting. Now what's even worse about the matter is that predators aren't born predators. Somewhere in that person's life, they faced some sort of trauma or abuse, or perhaps a situation that caused them to become who they are. Trauma can be generational. Trauma passed down through generations is called epigenetic inheritance. This type of heredity is linked to experiences and environments. It's a concept known as intergenerational transmission of trauma effects and has been shown to cause changes to a person's DNA. Black Americans technically have 400 years of epigenetic inheritance passed down from slavery. I come from a long line of trauma from my father's side.

Adverse Childhood Experiences (ACEs) also play a role in creating predators and victims. There are three types of ACEs, the first is abuse-which could be physical, mental, sexual, or even spiritual. The second is neglect, which could be physical and emotional. The third is a wide range category, which is household dysfunction, which can include incarceration of a parent, divorce, seeing your mother being abused, substance abuse (drugs or alcohol), mental illness, poverty, food insecurity, racism, and violence. So having an ACE score of six or more puts you at a heightened risk for health concerns. Therefore, trauma can affect you not only mentally but physically as well.

I have been writing this book since 2010. During that time, my youngest daughter was fighting cancer, and I was fighting a spiritual battle. I came face to face with my demons and I knew the time had come to finally stop running from them and face them head-on. I learned that fear was the fuel that demons use to torment me and I could no longer supply energy to them any further.

Every time I made an attempt to write my story, there was a distraction. Something was constantly sent in my path to keep me from writing. At first, it was financial blocks, but when that didn't work, the ammunition got heavier and heavier. I put my story on the back burner for some years after 2012. Me and my children had to move from California back to Las Vegas during my daughter's battle with cancer in fear of the hospital sending CPS (Child Protective Services) on me because I cured my baby of cancer with no chemo. That was frowned upon heavily in the social community and sometimes with members of society, including the government. So, we moved to Las Vegas and went into hiding for a bit.

In 2013 I got distracted selling cars and I didn't have time to write. But in 2019, I was fired from the car dealership I worked for, and I had to have a reparative surgery on my right hand. I was home and I had time to write. Just as I got in good with writing, the first tragedy struck. A main character in my book, the father of two of my children, was found dead at a hotel. For years he suffered from a drug addiction and for that reason, I couldn't allow him to have a relationship with his daughters. I wanted him to get better, I tried to motivate him by telling him as soon as he was clean, he could start being a part of their lives. But now the girls were in their 20's and pretty much the decision was up to them whether they wanted to pursue the relationship or not. Sadly, he overdosed because his crack was cut with fentanyl. He had been dead for a month before any of us found out.

There was a time I loved this man, but I couldn't be in love with him because of his addiction. He has an older daughter by another woman and she has been a part of our lives since the day we met her. The girls decided on having their father cremated and having a celebration of life ceremony for him at a place that he loved the most. The Griffith Park Observatory, located in Los Angeles, California. He used to take me there and we would hike up the hill and jump a fence to get to the Hollywood sign. We would look out at the entire city. I know why he loved it so much. It's one of the greatest views you'll ever see.

I didn't know how the girls would take his death seeing that they hadn't spent much time with him, but it crushed them. One of my daughters was hoping he could get himself clean enough to walk her down the aisle on her wedding day. My other daughter, who is usually pretty emotionless, was brought to tears, so I was crushed.

Once he was cremated, his ashes were given to the girls in a box. None of us had ever dealt with cremation, urns, or the handling of ashes so we were clueless. On the day of his celebration of life ceremony, the task of putting his ashes into the urn arrived. The girls were far too emotional to pour his ashes into the urn, so I had to step up and help out. I had no idea that when a body is cremated the weight of the ashes is so dense. I opened the box and looked inside. I saw bone fragments and teeth! I was horrified, but yet and still it had to be done.

Just as I positioned the urn to pour the ashes, - mind you we're outside, and it's a beautiful California day with not a bit of wind. But as I pour his ashes into the urn, out of nowhere a gush of wind blows and my ex's ashes, who just passed away from a drug overdose, blew right into my face! In my eyes, up my nose, and into my mouth! I froze!

On his last act on this earth, he decides to blow his ashes into me! I was so traumatized by this, I cried myself to sleep for three whole weeks. I

ANTECH

couldn't pull myself to write let alone do anything else at that time. And if that wasn't enough to spiral me back into a depression, aside from losing my job and losing the ability to use my right hand, someone very near and dear to me took his life.

This became a very dark time for me. As a mother, I felt I could never show my weaknesses. I always have to be strong for my family. I have to be the strength, the glue that holds the family together. Never a moment to be vulnerable. So, I quietly battled my demons.

My demons are known to me as the voice of suicide. This voice has been with me for most of my life. If you've never heard a voice telling you to kill yourself, consider yourself lucky. As I went through this battle, and I'm going to be very transparent, as recently as 2019, this voice came to me once again for the last time and tried to convince me to kill myself. This voice has no more power over me though.

You see, over the years, God has revealed Himself to me in ways that I can't explain to others. Since I was a child, I battled with suicidal thoughts and tendencies, but no one ever saw it. No one ever saw me. Only God kept me all these years from harming myself. But now as I have fought with all that is within me, victory belongs to me and the God in me!

So again, once I came out of my depression and made attempts to write again. At the end of 2019, I was blessed with the opportunity to open a business and that venture took my mind off everything. I felt so happy and full, owning and operating my own store, but I did so in the middle of a worldwide pandemic. The first year we did incredible for a new business opening up out of nowhere. The store stayed busy and we had so many wonderful community events. The connections and relationships that were built from that store are priceless, even to this day. But in 2022 my store went on a decline after a second round of COVID sent everyone into a panic and back to social distancing. As the store suffered, my family suffered a big loss. But that was just one of the many that you'll experience with me as you continue along my journey in the next few pages.

1. FORCES AGAINST ME

My story starts with me being a victim of my older brother from a very early age. Over the years we had no relationship, although I tried to create one with him for the sake of my family. But do you know what it feels like to look your abuser in the face on a constant basis? Then to have your mother tell you, that if you want to be a good Christian and get into Heaven you have to forgive this person and make things right with them? Most will never know. It was the most unfair statement ever made to me, but that's what was put into my head for years. So, I tried on a few occasions, but I just couldn't pull myself to like him, let alone love him.

The very last experience I had with him before his death was a family trip to Paris in 2016. The rest of my family stayed in an Airbnb but he and I got our own separate hotel rooms, at the same hotel. At check-in, there was a bit of confusion and his room was charged to my credit card. Once we got home, I called him, I said "Hey, that's crazy that the hotel messed up like that and charged your room to my card." He said "Yeah." So, I told him "Just send me the money and we'll be all good." But being the asshole that he was, he told me, "That ain't got nothing to do with me, that's between you the hotel, and your credit card company."

I asked him "What did you just say?" Then he said, "You a Big Baller, you got it!" I instantly felt anger surge through my body, but I tried to stay calm. I said, "It's really not that difficult, just send me my money." He told me "I'm not sending shit, take it up with whoever." So now the thug in me came out! I told him "If you don't send me my money Imma come right to your house and fuck up enough property to equal the amount charged on my card!" He asked, "Is that a threat?" I said, "No it's not a threat it's a muthafucken promise!" He had become another entity in my life that no longer ruled me through fear. That probably wasn't the best way to handle things but guess who got their money?

The words he said to me during this altercation were enough for me to decide I would never allow him a space in my life ever again to harm me. Anyway, I wrote him off and swore I would never speak to him again in life. When I got the call of his death, he as well, died in a hotel room and it took days or weeks for his body to be discovered. I was right in the middle of writing and ironically, I was writing about him.

I closed my laptop and put my story away for a year. My family knew it would only be a matter of time before this was to happen to him. Through the years, I often wondered how I would react when they told me he passed away. I knew I wouldn't have any emotion towards it, I only stopped writing because of what I was writing at the time I received the call of his passing.

Fast forward to 2024. This year has been a whirlwind and I have come across some good people and a great mentor who encouraged me to finish writing this book and to be as transparent as I can be. I was always afraid of transparency. I didn't want to hurt anyone's feelings, and I didn't want my children to be embarrassed of me or my story. I almost thought it would be best to not even write this book and just trash the entire idea of writing it. However, I have an amazing mentor who encouraged me to tell my story and to use my past to help others. Of course, nothing for me can ever be easy.

As I approached the end of writing this book, I was faced with yet another significant death. My oldest daughter's father tragically died in a motorcycle accident on June 25, 2024, the day after my youngest daughter's sixteenth birthday. That day my oldest daughter was boarding a plane to fly to Portugal, then to the Congo to be married.

She called me and I can always sense the tone in my children's voice when something is wrong. "Mommy" she shrilled. I instantly said, "What's wrong?" She said, "I don't know, I think my dad just died!" Earlier that day, someone I went on a few dates with, but then became a friend had killed five people and then killed himself, so I said to myself, "This can't be happening right now!"

She started crying "Please can you call my Grandma and see if it's true? My brother called me but it was a bad connection and I couldn't hear him!" I told her, "OK calm down, let me call her and I'll call you right back." Her Grandmother confirmed what I didn't want to hear. Honestly, I was messed up, because I had just returned home from California from the funeral of my third dad, then I was just processing the death of a friend from earlier that day, and then this! Three deaths all within two weeks. I called her and I had to give her the news that yes, her father had been killed in a motorcycle accident, only an hour apart from my friend's suicide.

Hearing my daughter cry out at the news of her father's passing as the door to the airplane shut and with no time for a decision to cancel her flight could be made was heart-wrenching. Not being able to be there to hold her and allow her to cry on my shoulder was crushing! All I could do was pray with her and I asked her to please look at how God orchestrated everything. God did not want her to cancel her travel plans! God wanted her to go through with her wedding. God is the best of planners and we have to learn how to accept His Will!

The three deaths I just spoke of are three people who hurt me the most during my life. I will admit that at this last death, I came to a clear revelation. Some may not like what I have to say, but I honestly believe that God used these three specific deaths to give me confirmation to tell my story. I, at one time in my life, loved each of these people. And I had to relearn how to love each of these individuals again, because I saw beyond the hurt that they had imparted on me and my life, and I saw their individual pain. That only came from a place that God showed me! God took me and showed me that energetically each and every one of us on this planet is connected. We all share the same energy source. When a person comes into our lives, our energy connects and crosses for a specific reason. We don't randomly come into someone's energy field for no reason. Our job on this planet is to understand what each person we encounter is in our life for!

Everyone you meet is either a lesson or a blessing! If we learn to not take people for granted, and we stop and analyze the union of that person, we will start to see things we would not normally see. We have to ask ourselves questions about people. Why are they here, what I am supposed to gain from this interaction? How does this improve, harm, or affect my life? Too often, we take people for granted! We abuse people when we sense weakness in them, just to selfishly empower ourselves. We want to feel smarter, stronger, and more important than others because it feeds our ego. But we just don't get it! Even if we feel a person who comes into our lives is inadequate in some way, we have to analyze the inadequacies. Because if we don't learn the lesson from that person, we will continue to meet that person in different forms throughout our lifetime. Then we'll ask ourselves "Why does every person that comes into my life act this way?" It's because you didn't learn the lesson from the first encounter!

I made the same mistakes in my life over and over again! Because I refused to see the lesson that the person in front of me was here to deliver. We all have something to teach someone be it good bad or indifferent, whether we know it or not. Some people are here to touch millions, some to touch thousands, hundreds, or tens. And some are here to touch just one. Imagine if you are the one somebody that person was meant to touch and you receive the message. You, personally will level up as a human being! Because you got the lesson. But now imagine you helped that person touch the one somebody they were meant to touch. That's life unlocked! Life isn't as complicated as we make it, we just have to learn to see people for who they are!

There's so much more to my story, so many stories left out. Most wouldn't be understood so I gave the surface level. Most names in this book have been changed to protect those involved, and some of the stories may have been slightly altered for reputation's sake.

2. DARK ENERGY

My life sure ain't no fairy tale! You won't see me dancing around the kitchen on any given weekday, preparing breakfast for my children as they quietly and patiently wait at the table for me to serve up some more pancakes. As I spin around the table in a dress fit for Doris Day, cheerfully singing a show tune! And you certainly won't see the Proverbial husband coming down the stairs dressed sharply in his suit getting ready to leave for work, as he dashes by each child giving them a loving kiss on the forehead. I walk him to the door with his lunch in my hands and he dips me to give me that "so long for now, but not Goodbye" kiss, and he waves to me with each step to the car as if it is agonizing to leave me just for the 10-hour workday. As he drives off, the kids scramble for their backpacks and lunch and run out the door for school, and I sit back and think about how much I love my life, my husband, my kids, and my home in the suburbs with the white picket fence in the front. Right! What a Fairy Tale! That cute life, that's not my story at all. I'm sure it's the life that all girls dream of, but I didn't get the fairy tale. Instead, I got the dark side, no, honestly, my story is very dark! A darkness I had to learn of the hard way!

How many times does this dark energy have to keep coming back to this world and reliving this life? Clearly, my energy has been a dark force for generations and it refused to see the light! Until me, that is! Is this my time? Will my dark side finally see the light this time around? I would guess my energy at some time was a child molester or a rapist. How else do you

5

come into this existence and be molested out of the gate? Starting life as a poor innocent soul, having done no harm to anyone. And yet being violated from the start. Being sexually assaulted, molested, and raped at a very young age, shapes and molds you for a future of dark sexual energy.

Before I turned 20, I had slept with almost 100 men. And no one knew. What drove me here? How did this become my life? What kind of life have I had? After all the therapy that I've been through you would think my issues would be resolved, but childhood trauma is a bitch, then expand that physical trauma with spiritual trauma, and you have a recipe for disaster. I had a crazy upbringing, but not the story people expect to hear from me. People who've known me most of my life are astonished when they hear some of the things I've experienced. Are my bad experiences a result of Generational Trauma? Or something even darker, more sinister!

Learning my family history was a pivotal part of learning myself. My paternal side of the family, the side I never knew, has dark secrets hidden deep in Louisiana. I had to go on a journey to New Orleans to learn the truth. The truth of who I am, and what secrets my family had hidden in an unmarked grave in Bogalusa, Louisiana. What I learned is that I come from a long line of trauma. My great-great-grandfather was a white man, who married a black woman. This was in the late 1700s, and his family wasn't too happy about that, so while his siblings received land in his father's will, he received a bed of feathers. This man is the father of my great-grandmother Lena Elizabeth.

Through my dreams and revelations, I learned that my great-grandmother, Lena, who was half Igbo, dabbled with dark energy. In records I obtained on my grandmother, Ellestine, I learned she was abused by my great-grandfather, JWB Smith, and my grandfather, John Smith. Let me explain. Ellestine's parents passed away when she was a teen. She and her sisters inherited her family land. They were adopted by a pastor and his wife in the church, Surname Baptiste. Ironically my great-grandfather was a preacher. He had a son who was the same age as the recently orphaned teen who had just inherited land. Perfect, they will get married. My grandfather, Johnny builds a home on the land and then goes off to the military. There is no way this young girl can manage this home and land alone, so the preacher, JWB, and Lena move Ellestine into their home.

During the marriage of my grandparents, Ellestine gave birth to 2 sons, one of which is my father. My grandmother started to endure abuse at the hands of the men in the house. That abuse eventually drove her crazy and she was committed to a mental hospital and diagnosed as being Catatonic Schizophrenic. Based on letters and reports that I obtained, written from the mental institution where she was housed, the abuse she suffered at the hands of these men was so severe that she didn't want to leave the hospital when they would try to come and get her. When she returned to the hospital after weekend visits, she would be dirty and malnourished, and her mental state would be worsened. During a weekend visit at home, she becomes pregnant again and she has a daughter. Same scenario, but different date, another weekend visit, she became pregnant a fourth time and gave birth to another daughter while in the mental hospital. Lena came and took the baby, while she already had her other 3 children, and raised them as her own. My grandmother, Ellestine died, alone in the mental hospital at 35 years old, and was put in an unmarked grave in Bogalusa LA.

Ever since I was very young, I had two women speaking to me in my dreams. I used to wake up in fright crying that two witches were after me. I recently discovered the two witches I have experienced my whole life were my Great-Grandmother Lena and my Grandmother Ellestine. Why did these women choose me to communicate with? Maybe because my name is a fusion of the two women El-Lena. They have been battling each other, trying to convince me that each other is a witch!

I took a trip to Louisiana and I discovered some truths, but much more than that was revealed. Ellestine has been trying to communicate with me my whole life. She only wanted her story to be known and had it not been for a dream, I would have never gone on this journey. In my dream, the setting had to be the early 1900s. It was a beautiful day; the sun was shining. A car was driving down a winding dirt road with a well-dressed, black couple in the front seats. The man driving wore a nice suit, and the woman in the passenger seat was in a beautiful ruffled dress, with a matching hat. In the back seat sat two cute black teenage girls, also dressed in fancy white dresses and their hair in cute ponytails with white ribbons. The girls playfully laughed with each other.

Suddenly out of nowhere, the father notices a mob of white men, holding shotguns, standing in the middle of the road and he swerves to avoid hitting them. The car hits a tree killing the man and the woman instantly, but projecting the girls out of the car and into a lake that sat at the side of the road. I woke up from my dream.

When I went to bed the next night, I was compelled to see the dream again, so I put my moonstone crystal in my right hand and asked to return to the dream. First, I saw a bunch of colors swirling around in my head. Then I went back to the dream, but instead of being projected into the water, the two girls stood at the riverbank with the mob of white men around them. The older-looking girl was pulled into the water by a white man, while she cried. Then the second girl holds her head up with a stern look on her face and walks into the water. As she enters the water a circle of blood starts coming from her and covering her white dress, now she's standing in a circle of blood in the water, she looks in horror and starts screaming or crying.

All the men around her are pointing and laughing at her. Just then a woman in a black hooded cloak is hovering above the scene and the men stop laughing and they scramble and run. She looks directly at me and says: Yes, I am a Red Witch, but I'm not the one who will harm you! You were selected, your name was carefully selected, it holds meaning, you are THE LIGHT! You have a power that you don't yet understand. You are not who you want to be because you don't believe you are worthy of being it. You have to understand your power. SHE (as she points to the young girl covered in blood) didn't want to accept it! SHE believed THEM instead of ME. SHE is THE DARK and SHE thinks she's helping you but she's not. You have to serve your purpose. Lena is the Red Witch and Ellestine is in the white dress in the lake.

3. EARLY BEGINNINGS

As a child, I was abused and neglected. Not the brutal abuse faced by some, but everyone's perception of their own experience differs. Although I had parents in the home, I was raised by my siblings. Pretty much we raised ourselves. I know that was pretty common in my era of growing up, but I had demons in my house. I've had to dig deep into my life, to answer my questions of why? Why did I have to go through what I went through? Why did I do the things that I did? What's the explanation for my behaviors? And more importantly, my questions about my Spirituality, what is my purpose and what is God trying to tell me? Why am I always the BLACK SHEEP? And who keeps hitting their head against the same wall continuously in life as I have?

It has taken me 54 years and I'm just learning that life is love, but how do you learn to love when you've never known a real, good love? And how do you learn to love when your life has been filled with so much abuse? How do you learn to love someone whom you hate so much? Someone who has hurt you so deep to your core that it changed your whole life or changed who you are and who you could have been. You never know who you could have been if certain things had never happened to you. I wanted to know love my whole life, but I've been confused about what love really is.

I've always confused love with sex or lust, not knowing what true love is. I never thought with my mind only through impulse and never listened to the good voice of reason in my head. I know as a little girl I never once said "When I grow up, I want to be a single baby mama with 5 kids, struggling to survive". I don't recall that thought, but what I do recall is dysfunction. I'm not uneducated, wasn't raised in the ghetto, on the contrary, I grew up with two employed, hard-working parents in the home. I don't have the typical, "I was born a poor black child" story. In the seventies, two working parents put you in the Middle Class.

I was born on November 30th, 1969 4:41 am at John Wesley Hospital in Inglewood California. I was born coded. My birthdate, 11-3-6-9, and my birth time 4+4+1=9 are significant Gematria numbers. My name, El means The or God, and Lena means Light. What's in a name? Most times our parents name us and they, themselves don't understand the power of a name! Numbers guide us into our next existence if we learn their coding. I have memories that go back to maybe 1 year old. I remember being a baby in an apartment, we had a green sofa that was covered in hard plastic. Above the sofa was a black felt painting with a colorful abstract of a sailboat. I remember looking up at the painting and staring at it.

We had a floor TV and I remember standing at eye level to it. I also remember touching the TV and my father popping my hand. But my memory was opened to go further back than that! You see I opened my Akashic records, and just by asking I saw my energy throughout time. I saw myself as a white racist woman, who got hit by a car and died the day of my birth. Before that, I saw myself as a white racist slave owner that yes raped his slaves. I saw myself as an African King who had slaves. I even saw myself as various animals and as an Egyptian. Sounds crazy right? I can't explain how or why I get the visions and dreams that I do, but I know I learned how to open portals at a very young age, and it can be considered a blessing and a curse.

At the time of my birth, my family lived in Watts CA. My birth father was from Louisiana, he was a very handsome, brown skin brotha, very suave and debonaire. He was the playboy type, everyone loved him and he loved to go clubbing. He was the life of the party, he drank and used drugs. He worked odd jobs after the Military and eventually opened his own business. He was a hands-on father, such as camping trips, he took us swimming and he took my brothers to play sports at the YMCA. But he had his "demons";

that monkey on his back, Unresolved Generational Trauma.

My mother comes from two of the most loving people to walk the face of the earth, but they were quick to pull out that switch. Her parents lived in Boley, OK. In the early 1900s. Boley was an all-black town, with black banks, black stores, and black businesses. When I was little my grandfather would tell me stories of how he and the other townsmen sat on the roof of a building, guns drawn, and ran off Pretty Boy Floyd's band of robbers, who thought they were going to roll into Boley and pull off a bank heist. True Thugs! She is black and Native American, so she was very pretty as a young woman. She was a wild one in her days; I've heard some of her stories. She also liked to party and drink!

After her family left Boley they moved to Oakland, CA., and because the crime was so terrible there, they settled in Sacramento, CA. She met my father in Northern Cali and they moved to Southern Cali. She became the breadwinner of the family; she worked at a security company and held a good position there. She played the classy role very well. Always sharply dressed, closet full of clothes and shoes, and make-up done to a Tee. She also has some Unresolved Trauma that she will take to the grave with her.

I only know that my dad abused my mom from the stories that I've heard. I was too young to remember, but my mom and sisters talked about it quite often. Well mostly my sisters, because my dad was abusive to them. And they remember images of him physically abusing my mother. Hitting her or dragging her down the hall by her hair. I'm glad that I don't have those memories. But I know my father was a monster and a rapist. It's hard to say that, but he raped a young girl. He was arrested, in front of our home for rape. Of a 14-year-old girl by knifepoint. What type of monster does that? One that fights demons and has no idea of the fight he is facing. As a child I was in love with my father and no one could speak badly about him. But learning the truth and accepting it are the most mature things you could ever do in life!

The dynamics of our family are a little peculiar, but everyone has their skeletons. My oldest sister, my second brother, and I share the same mother and father. Then there are the twins. Second in birth order, but they have a different father than us. Apparently, when my dad was away in the military my mom cheated on him, or they broke up and she entered into a new relationship in his absence, with an older dark-skinned Military man. We only knew he was dark-skinned because the twins have a darker complexion than the three of us, which always caused a problem between the sisters in our house. Always a competition between us, even before I realized what was going on.

My father came home and accepted the twins as his own, and went on to marry my mother and have me and my brother. I would assume that's where the abuse starts. My mom worked long hours and my dad, well he spent most of his time partying. My brother and I were raised by our older siblings. Around the time I turned two, our family moved from Watts to Azusa CA, a suburb in the lower San Fernando Valley. It was an all-white racist neighborhood. I remember the day we moved there. I remember the moving truck in our new driveway and my dad and his friend taking our things off the truck and into our new house, but more importantly, I remember all our white neighbors standing outside on their porches, watching our black family move into their white neighborhood. It wasn't the warm welcome my mom was expecting. When we moved to Azusa my mom got the courage to put my dad out of the house. He and our dog Fluffy were kicked out. I cried over losing Dad and the dog even though I couldn't stand Fluffy, he chased me every time I stepped foot in the backyard!

Me and my siblings had the typical black family upbringing. Saturday morning cartoons over a bowl of cereal, then Soul Train and American Bandstand, followed by old school music like Al Greene and our Chores, then outside to play until the street lights came on. My older siblings had to take on lead roles around the house. My older sister was supposed to hold the title of cook when my mom went to work. Growing up, she was the one responsible for making sure dinner was cooked, and that was just way too much responsibility for her. She always burned the food, then she would flip out, always on some kind of an emotional rollercoaster, so every other week she ran away. Then she would come home, take her whooping, and go back to business as usual.

My second sister, the oldest girl twin, has always had an issue with her complexion, as she claims, "Growing up as a dark-skinned girl between two light-skinned sisters was hard". But that was shocking to hear because as a little girl, I used to wish I looked like her. She has the most beautiful dimples and perfect teeth! I always thought she was so beautiful, and I loved her skin color, so I don't and won't understand what she goes through. She has a hard personality, almost masculine, everyone always thought she was the older sister because she's so controlling. She has always had a smart mouth, especially when it came to my mom. She was quick to talk back and could make up a lie so good she believed it herself and convinced herself that it was the truth!

I always looked up to her, because my mom worked so much, that she just took over the role of Mother in the house. Making sure we ate, and that we did our homework, got to bed on time. She got so into character that she even went to parent conferences, unannounced to my actual Mother. She and Mom always bumped heads, I think she actually started to believe that she was the woman of the house, but what could my mom say, she wasn't there!

The other twin was a boy and I can't remember a time that I liked him. He was always so mean, and his face was always twisted. He never had a smile on his face, just bitterness and evil. He always fought with my sisters when my mom was gone, and I don't mean arguing, I mean throwing sharp objects, like knives or screwdrivers at them, or aerosol cans being thrown behind the stove blowing up the kitchen type of fights. He was so mean to everyone in our house. I was always scared of him; he was such a negative energy in the family!

Then there was the younger, but older than me, brother. I always felt I had to speak for him or protect him, even when he didn't want me to. He was very afraid of my mom. She basically "bullied" him because she knew he was afraid of her. He stuttered in her presence because she never spoke to him, she just spoke down to him. I think she didn't like him because he reminded her of our Father, he looks just like him. I hated how she treated him. He was my best friend in our house. We played together, went to the park together, and got into trouble together. I also looked at him as MY protector.

And then there's me the baby. Spoiled little bratty sister, yet charming and cute. Regardless of what pain I went through in life I was always goofy and was laughing on the outside while I screamed and cried on the inside. I have always had a strong spiritual connection with God even as a little girl. I have always dreamed of events and then seen them on the news, like plane crashes or earthquakes. I faced a lot of issues growing up, but because of my connection with God, it kept me sane. I always wonder how would I have turned out if I had a normal life. I only know now that God was shaping and molding me through tragedy.

I really loved my dad and his leaving was a sad time for me even at two years old, but I had no idea what kind of abuse was going on in our home. If my dad ever did anything sexual to me, I wouldn't remember because I was too young, but I have such early memories of being exposed to sexual things. I have memories of being very young and being put in compromising situations, such as other little boys laying on me and pretending to have sex with me. Whether it was our babysitters' sons or cousins, I just know I was exposed young.

When my older sister got to an age where my mom felt we didn't need a babysitter any longer, me and my brother were put in the care of our older siblings. It seems to me, that just as my biological father walked out the door my stepfather came through it. I just remember seeing a strange man in a red robe, in the kitchen cooking bacon! He stepped into the home of a single woman with 5 children. My Mom was a hard-working woman and a strong disciplinarian. Honestly, she was very abusive to us. She was quick with the belt and definitely did not spare the rod. We all feared her, and that's what she wanted!

She thrived on us fearing her, so she could cut one look at us and we would instantly stand at attention. I understand children having a healthy fear of their parents, that can be a life-saving tactic. But alongside discipline has to be love and that's the part she missed. She was the Momma that came home from work at 2 in the morning and would violently wake all of us up to beat that ass if the house was out of order and she did this at least once, sometimes twice a week. She didn't discriminate on the beatings; although I was probably beaten the least of anyone in the house,

I was very traumatized by this experience. Sometimes she would call us in the middle of the day from work and tell us we were getting a whopping when she got home from work, so I couldn't sleep in fear of getting beat when she got home. I used to pray that she would have a car accident on the way home. Most times our whopping's were unjustified!

4. LITTLE GIRL LOST

Our new stepdaddy was fun and he tried to lighten things up a bit around the house, always joking and singing, and he had the foulest mouth you ever heard. F this and MF that, he sounded like Richard Pryor, but when he moved in, my older siblings wanted no part of this new male figure in the house, except me, I was the youngest and I loved him. He appeared to me as "Superman", well that's what I kept calling him. "Superman, Superman, is that your car?" I would ask him about his Volkswagen Bug. He did fun things with us like taking us to the park or the mountains. At first, the older kids were angry at his very presence. Mad at my mom for kicking our real Dad out, and allowing this imposter to come in his place. But after a while, the girls lightened up to him.

My older brother was especially mad, because my dad was the only father he knew and he hated to see him leave, and he wanted revenge on my mother for putting dad out. First came his destructive behavior, you know like destroying her things: flowers, trinkets whatever he could get his hands on. Then came violent behavior at school, fights, running with gangs, and drinking, and then ultimately drug use. All this started at the young age of 10, it could have been younger, and yes in the suburbs. A lot of it started in Watts, you think you're going to move your kids to a better neighborhood, but if your kids want trouble, they can always find it no matter where you move to.

I always knew my brother hated me. He would sneer at me and he

16

would constantly call me white girl. That would make me burst into tears because I couldn't stand white people at the time because of what I was going through at school. He was very mean to me and everyone in the house. He spent most of his time thinking of ways to antagonize me and my sisters. Constantly making jokes about us, and saying things to entice fights, he was a whole menace. The worst of his behavior was yet to come, and why oh why did I have to be his victim? I didn't do anything to him; I thought he was mad at Mom. Well, I *was* her baby. And she *did* treat me a little bit differently than she did with the other kids. So, in his little devious mind, the best way to get back at her was to hurt something or someone that she appeared to like more than the others.

It started with physical abuse, he would hit me or try to scare me by locking me in the linen closet, that's probably why I'm so claustrophobic now, but I would cry to Mom and he would get in trouble. But he didn't care about getting in trouble, he got daily whopping's or was constantly on restriction, so none of that mattered to him. Then his opportunity came knocking. A chance for his demons to really show their face!

Growing up, our family was one of the few black families in the white suburban town of Azusa. There were quite a few Mexican families, but our family was one of three black families in the whole town. I was called nigger so much I thought I was one. The teachers treated me badly; they acted like they didn't want to touch me. And if I told the teacher that one of the kids called me a nigger, she would make them write it on the board 100 times, now every kid in class is reading the board out loud, "nigger nigger nigger nigger nigger!"

The kids would call us Jungle Bunnies and tell us to go back to Africa. I was bullied on a daily basis at school. It was a terrible situation for us. I always thought I was ugly because that's what they told me daily. I was asked if the dirt on my skin washed off, and the white kids asked me if I even took a bath! They would say "You have nappy hair and big lips", hearing that got old, so my self-esteem was in the toilet! Our next-door neighbors were white and they accepted us but were ridiculed for that. They were called the "nigger lovers". I would sometimes go to their house and play dolls with their younger daughter, and we went over there on occasion to watch movies or swim in their pool, although I could tell their father despised us coming into the house.

They had a creepy son that my brother had befriended. He was older than me but not quite as old as my brother. And for some reason, I would play with him outside by myself and no one thought anything of it. I played a lot by myself in the backyard. I had two imaginary friends that I used to play with, Tracy and Monty, pretty mature names for imaginary friends, but that's what they told me their names were, so I spent a lot of time alone in the backyard playing with them.

I always thought my neighbor was weird, he would do strange things like pee on this electric fence that was in their yard, he would kill lizards and set them on fire, or light up a tennis ball with lighter fluid and throw it at me and my brother as we ran down the side of the house screaming! Sometimes he would just come randomly poop in our backyard, and all I could think to myself even as a young child, was he's a nasty ass white boy! But none of that could have prepared me for what he did to me!

One day when I was 5 years old, we were outside playing and he started peeing on the side of our shed in the backyard. When I saw him peeing, I turned around and took off running. He ran after me, pinned me down, sat on my chest, and put his nasty little pink penis in my mouth. And if that's not the most disgusting thing you could ever imagine, he still had urine on his penis when he put it in my mouth and I could taste it. I tried to spit the urine taste out of my mouth and I started wiggling to try to get him off me, I was so repulsed.

As I wiggled, he pinned me down and was attempting to rape me, trying to pull my pants down. I didn't understand what was happening to me and I think that's why I didn't scream, but thankfully we heard footsteps coming into the backyard. It was my older brother, so he quickly jumped off me and pulled his pants up. Clearly, my brother saw what was happening to me, but do you think he protected me? Of course not, instead of protecting me, my brother used that to blackmail me!

The very next day, right after that tragic event happened to me, while I was in my room playing dolls, my brother came to me and told me "I know what you did with the neighbor yesterday, and if you don't do it to me, I'm gonna tell Mama that you was doing nasty stuff with him"! I tried to tell my brother what happened, but he cut me off and said "If I tell Mama on you she's going to give you a whopping!" I was confused by what he was saying to me. Did he really want me to put his thing in my mouth? Ewww! But, out of the fear I had for my mother, I did what he told me to do.

My brother didn't make me do it once, he made me do it the next day, and the day after that, and the day after that! Then the days turned to weeks and the weeks turned to months, and then to years. I tried to pretend this wasn't happening to me, so I tried to act as normal as possible because I didn't want anyone to find out. Out of nervousness, I would laugh uncontrollably, I don't know why, maybe laughing to keep from crying. Most days I would just stay in my room and play with my dolls or my easy bake oven, I was too afraid to be in the backyard by myself. When a child is exposed to sexual arousal it takes away every bit of your youth and innocence that a child is supposed to consist of.

Every chance he got my brother made me perform oral sex on him, and he would lay on me and put his penis on my vagina and grind on me. After that, I started to feel sexual urges as a five-year-old child. It was a nauseating feeling, and I was so scared to tell anyone because he always threatened me. When this first started, I was in kindergarten and he was in continuation school, so he got home before the other kids. My mom worked from the afternoon to late at night, so as he and I would come home, around 1:30 pm, she was leaving out the door to work.

I just remember crying to her not to leave me, but she would just walk out the door and didn't pay any attention to my crying. My school would call her and tell her that my behavior was strange and that I was always in the office, maybe because they would let the kids bully me and wouldn't stop them! But all my behavior was strange, I started peeing on myself in class, on the way home from school, and at night in bed. But I don't think she even noticed anything. She was so wrapped up in her job and her new man she didn't have any time for her kids and we all had to become self-sufficient.

Then my mom and stepdad started taking weekend trips to Las Vegas. I always looked forward to the weekends because everyone was home and I didn't have to be alone with my brother. The weekend was the only time I saw my mom, and now they're leaving almost every weekend. I didn't know it then but stepdaddy had a major gambling problem. If he wasn't in Vegas, he was at Santa Anita horse races and if he wasn't at the horse races, he was at a pool hall, and if he wasn't at a pool hall he was somewhere betting on a game. My life felt like a disaster. I know my mom didn't enjoy being a mom. We got in the way of her new life. I would sit by her bedroom door waiting for her to wake up some mornings just so I could look at her and see if she still existed, other than the monster that came home in the middle of the night to wake us up just so she could find a reason to whip us, on a school night no doubt. The only time she ever told us that she loved us was when she was drunk and slurring her words. This was Hell, and I didn't want to be here.

5. GLASS HOUSE FAMILY

On the outside our family appeared so normal. We had the house in the suburbs, the cute little Pinto (a five-seater car for a family of 7). Two working parents, my older sisters were cheerleaders, my brothers played Little League. It all looked good, but our house was dysfunctional on the inside. My sisters both had their own issues, my mother and stepfather were drinking heavily, and my oldest brother, well you know, everything was wrong with him. And then there was me and the younger brother, Ken.

Because he had a hard time communicating with my mother, he stuttered when he talked to her, she was so mean to him. She would beat him just because. She would claim that he did or didn't do something even if he did or didn't do it. She was the judge, the jury, and the executioner. If she said you were wrong, even if you weren't proven guilty, you were wrong, it didn't matter to her. Off with your head! We never could understand her. We always had to question her love for us. She never saw herself as being as abusive as she was. If we questioned her love she would break out in fake tears, then she would become very intimidating, and she used fear as a tactic against us. After, she would force us to say we love her, she would have all of us line up and she made us kiss her on the cheek, as she blew cigarette smoke in our faces. Some creepy Mommy Dearest type shit!

I learned how to play her game and I played her very well, basically, I kissed her ass! Hey, I watched everyone getting their nightly ass whopping so I figured if I was nice to her and said nice things to her, maybe she wouldn't be so harsh with me, and it worked. I would tell her "Mommy I love you" or "Mommy you're so pretty", so I could stay on her good side, but I had mixed emotions about her. She was so weird because that type of groveling love was what she wanted. I was so torn, I loved her because she was my mom and she *did* take me to eat or to get ice cream when she wouldn't take the others, but I hated her for being so mean, and whipping Ken so much. That was my best friend growing up and to see him get in trouble all the time for no reason didn't sit very well with me. But I had to protect myself also so I played the role.

I was also mad at her because I felt that I had given her more than enough signals to let her know that something was wrong with me, but she didn't pick up on any of them! I always had a stomach ache or a headache. I didn't want to go to school, I didn't want to be home. She completely ignored me and paid absolutely no attention to what was going on in her home. She spent her life with stepdaddy, and they were gone more and more. For a while my biological father would come and visit us. He would take us out for the day to visit with his family in LA, but his visits started to become scarce. He would call and say he was on his way, and I would sit by the door all day, waiting for him to come. I wouldn't even go outside to play for fear of messing up my clothes. But I would fall asleep by the door waiting for him and he would never show up. Then after a while, he stopped calling!

As time went by Mom and stepdad spent more time going away for the weekend. They got married in Las Vegas, and the only way we found out was when my mom put the wedding pictures up in the den. We were shocked! When did they get married? And why weren't we invited? This was cold, we really were not a part of her life. My older siblings were out of control. Always having people over, throwing parties, and me and Ken was right in the middle of it all. There was always alcohol and drugs at their parties. I started tasting alcohol at a very young age. I remember me and Ken being drunk at some of those parties.

My oldest sister started hanging around an older girl who stole anything she got her hands on and we followed right along with them. There was rebellion and uprising in the house. The older girls were sneaking

22

out all the time to go party, and my older brother was all over the place, making bad drug deals with local gang members. He was always high and always in trouble. I hated him! Just looking at him made my stomach churn. When he would come into the house, I would instantly get sick. When I moved up to regular school hours, I thought things would get better because Ken would be around to protect me from him, but it didn't happen. He just made him be a lookout for my sisters. When was this going to stop?

God, please protect me, is what I used to pray at night. I was having nightmares; I was an insomniac and I would always hyperventilate. I remember around the time I turned 6 I was constantly touching myself. I would lay on the sofa watching cartoons and my hand was always in my panties. I remember my stepfather walked by the den and saw me and he yelled at me "Get your hands out your pants!" But shouldn't that have been a red flag? Isn't that something that would require an investigation? Nothing was said to me, so I would do it in private and make sure no one was watching me.

My family always thought I was just being a drama queen because I was always sick. My mom told me to stop faking sick because I had the school calling her every other day, I was always in the office with a headache. I developed several trauma responses. This may sound crazy but I learned how to astro plane out of my body, so I didn't have to be present for the abuse. Literal astro plane, like I would float above my body, then out the door to the neighbor's house, to the top of the tree in their yard and watch everything going on in the neighborhood.

I only knew it was real because I would see Ken coming home from baseball practice, walking and tossing his ball in the air, then dropping it and retrieving it. Before he would come through the door, I would jump back into my body. At first, I thought I was just daydreaming, but soon realized it was a real occurrence, based on the time he would walk through the door. I thought I was going crazy, but I loved the feeling of being detached. Being able to Astro Plane also unlocked the door for dark energies to see me and hear me.

For as long as I can remember I heard voices in my room. Two witches used to sit in the corner of my room and watch me sleep. In the beginning, I would belt down the hallway to my mother's room screaming my head off! My stepdad would take me back to my room, turn on the lights, and toss up my bed to reassure me no one or nothing was there. But they were there every night and eventually, I got used to them being there. Now I don't know if you're familiar with Succubus, but he is a dark sexual energy. I came to know him early on in life. He felt inclined to violate me constantly since that portal on me had already been opened. I was being molested in the physical and the spiritual and it started when I was only 5!

That's when the dream started. I'm about 5 years old every time in the dream. I would be in a room or a chamber, and the floor was wet with either water or blood, I couldn't tell the difference because red would pulsate through the whole room. I'm sitting on the floor handcuffed to a metal chair that is welded to the ground. I'm sitting there in a little white gown, shivering from fear. In the corner is a huge, dark beast, with his back to me, breathing hard and slightly growling. The beast turns around and starts to slowly walk toward me. As he stands over me, slobber is dripping on me from his mouth, and then suddenly he violently grabs me and throws me down, tears off my panties, and very aggressively performs oral sex on me. I cover my face as tears stroll down my face, but it happens on such an occasional basis that I am no longer screaming, I guess I kind of get used to being used in this way. I have this dream way more often than I want to.

As I got older, I had enough of being molested. I wanted my brother to stop touching me and making me do sexual things to him. So, about the time I turned 11 (yes, this crap went on this long) when he would come to me, he would tell me to go to his room and I would just start crying and would not stop, and I got louder and stooped in a corner. He just looked at me and would walk away. I had to do this several times and after a while he stopped.

Man, if I would have known that was all it would take to make him stop, I would have done that a long time ago. One day as I lay in the grass in my front yard, a very strange phenomenon occurred. It was a clear sunny day, but out of nowhere a large white fluffy cloud appeared in the sky, and then the cloud quickly moved over me. I put my finger up in the air and I could feel the coolness of the cloud touch my finger. Then a voice told me, "Don't ever fear, a lot will come to scare you but just know I'm always here!" That gave me a feeling as though I was being watched and looked after.

When my brother stopped molesting me, he became very violent towards me and everyone in the house. My mom was fighting him like he was some dude on the streets. She was throwing Mike Tyson blows on him. Drop kicking him out of chairs, breaking rulers across his back, switches, belts, cords! It was so crazy to watch. She would kick him out of the house and he would sneak back in when she went to work. He would live in the garage and she didn't even know. My older sisters were so over raising me, they hated every bit of being responsible for me, and who could blame them?

They hated getting me dressed for school in the morning, they hated combing my hair. Some mornings when I was in kindergarten they would leave out and not look at me and forget to comb my hair. I had to pull dirty clothes out of the hamper most of the time to wear to school, and often I would just put the same thing on day after day. I went to school looking crazy, like an uncared-for orphan. I was just a baby; I didn't know any better.

As I got a little older like 10 or 11, my sisters had me running the streets with them and their crazy friends. I had to go with them, they had no choice. I had been stealing with them and tried to look older than my age. I would flirt with their boyfriends and had crushes on boys twice my age. I was kissing boys at church and talking to them on the phone all the time. My mom didn't know and probably didn't care. She never checked on me, she didn't even check to see if I was doing homework or how I was doing in my classes. She was not there for me! Because I kept my grades up, she felt I didn't need her to monitor me, but she was on Ken's ass and because his grades were failing and he stuttered, the school put him in a learning program. So, she beat the learning into him. That was the only good thing that came from her beatings because if she hadn't done that, he wouldn't have learned the way he did. Everyone in the house required her attention except me, the one who needed it the most! I was constantly fighting kids at school because I had enough of being called out my name!

Even on the weekends on her off days, rather than spending time with us, she sent us to this all-white racist Christian Church by ourselves, on a church bus. Once we realized how out of place we were there, we would get off the bus and walk to Burger King where we would use our offering money to buy French fries and kick back until it was time to go home. This church was another example of places we didn't belong! One of the ladies at the church told us in Sunday school that Jesus loves even the little black children. That's where she sent us! She never went to that church with us, she didn't go to church at all until one night, we had a tire blowout on the freeway and my mom claimed she "saw her life flash before her eyes" and suddenly she turned all religious on us.

So, she found a black church in Monrovia and she made us go to church all day on Sunday for service, Monday for the general meeting, Wednesday for Bible study, Thursday for CYF, and Saturday for choir rehearsal, while she only went on Sunday. There was an older woman in the church who would pick us up for all these services and take us home on the weekdays because my mom was still working crazy hours. It was too much church. Now the church was trying to raise us!

We were some out-of-control kids. The church kids were bad as hell, but at least we were with other black children. All the little boys at church were flirting with me, trying to kiss me. I was growing up so fast and my mom never talked to me about boys. We never had any conversation about respecting yourself as a young lady. Hell, I was already exposed to sex so it meant nothing to me. There were no boundaries, I thought kissing boys and letting them touch on you was a normal thing. At this time, I was eleven years old!

6. CRUMBLING DOWN

My older brother was still running crazy around Azusa, then he beat up some Mexican gang member and broke his jaw. The guy was in the hospital, but his friends came to our house in the middle of the night and started shooting. Then a group of guys came to our door and demanded money from my parents to pay for the drugs that my brother never paid for. We had to move, and we had to move quickly!

My older sister was pregnant with her first child and her baby was born with calcium deposits on his brain, he was born severely disabled, but he was the most beautiful baby ever and I was so in love with him. We moved to the High Desert, to a nice big home on the hill in Victorville, CA. There were actually Black people in Victorville! I grew up all my life around white kids and Mexicans, I was so excited to finally go to school with kids that looked like me and wouldn't call me nigger or jungle bunny. The first day of school I was so excited, but then all I heard from these kids was that I talked like a white girl. I couldn't believe it; I was being discriminated against by my own people. They gave me funny looks and called me stuck up, and in the first week of my new school, I got into a fight! I instantly hated Victorville.

Now stepdad had three kids from his previous marriage, and we would see them on occasion, but when we moved to Victorville guess who moved in??? All three of them, now it was us five kids, my sister's new baby, and Mom and stepdad! We had a full house and it was so chaotic. My stepsister was a major thief, we robbed the local Circle K blind. And my stepbrothers, one of them cussed just as bad as his dad and the other was money hungry, which helped me and Ken out because at first, we would do the dishes for the older kids for a slice of cheese and a pickle, but he opened our eyes, he would tell us "You can walk in the kitchen any time you want and grab a pickle and some cheese. You better start charging them money," and our hustle was on!

But yet and still it was too many people under one roof, so my mom first got rid of my oldest sister and her baby. She found her a small apartment in the ghetto, affordable enough even for her meager welfare check. Then the stepkids, not only were they living with us, but stepdad was still paying child support to their mother. Our finances were going downhill, and my stepdad was still working near Azusa, quite a long drive from Victorville. Finally, my mom got the Governor and a Congressman to read one of her numerous letters about the stepkids living with us while their mom was collecting child support, food stamps, welfare, and owned a business, so the kids moved back home.

But by this time my parents had loans on top of loans that they couldn't repay. My stepdad was the only one working; my mom quit her job when we moved and tried to become a mom, but it was kind of too late for that. No one in the house respected or even liked her. Our finances started to dwindle. Mom's car broke down and stepdad had to stay in the city during the week to get to work, so we had no car for driving around Victorville.

When we moved to the Ville it didn't take my older brother long to create a name for himself and to find trouble. He confronted the guy who was known to be the biggest and the baddest of Victorville, and in front of the whole school, he beat his ass! After that, every girl in town thought this asshole was the shit! I had girls at my Jr. high school asking if he was my brother and if I wanted to eat lunch with them! My answer was "ABSOLUTELY NOT" I definitely wasn't going to make friends on his name! He became the small-town celebrity, he was cutting school and coming home high every day, and my mom finally had enough. One day he came home high off his ass, he started fighting with everyone in the house, and then he punched his twin in the eye. He and my mom got into the roughest fight I had ever seen, she kicked him out, and this time HE WAS GONE FOR GOOD! He ended up getting his GED and got into the military. His twin graduated high school and she went into the Air Force. Everyone was gone except my parents, Ken, and me.

You would think life would get peaceful at this point, but it didn't! We were so broke. We couldn't afford food or clothes; we had no car and the utilities kept getting turned on and off. My grandmother bought my mom a bucket. My sis in the Military sent money all the time, but why were we always so broke? Maybe because my stepdad was gambling all the money away!!!! Here we are struggling and he is gambling, and his gambling turned into a real problem. My grandmother bought clothes for me and Ken, and we wore those same clothes for three years. Luckily my older sis got a job and I started babysitting my nephew. I had to use my babysitting money to buy school clothes for me and Ken, so I thought what the hell! I'll just steal clothes. Kmart and Pic and Save were the easiest targets, so I stole everything that I could get my hands on. Ken and I got smart, we started using our lunch money to buy candy at Smart & Final, to sell at school, or sometimes steal candy to sell at school. We had a whole business and soon all the kids knew us for having all the snacks.

Most summers we would go up to Northern Cali and stay with my grandmother or my aunt, and I had a cousin who was a few years older than us, but she was into so much. She and her friends smoked weed and drank all the time, so about the time I was twelve my cousin was getting me and my brother high. Her friends thought it was the funniest thing to get us high then take us into public places and watch us act a fool and embarrass ourselves. One time they got us high and we went to hang out at her high school. There was a teacher-staff meeting taking place and they dared me to stand on the table the teachers were sitting at and sing "I don't care what the white man says Santa Claus is a nigga!" And my fool ass did it! We grew up with the best influences. SMH

By this time, I had made some friends in Victorville, and we would steal alcohol and get drunk, this was in Jr. High. I was drinking, and stealing. On some days my older sis would come and get me from school because I was always sick. I would call her and tell her that I wanted to go home and she would come to get me, and instead of taking me home she would say "Let's go shopping", which was code word for stealing, and that was cool to me. She never told my mom; we would just go hang out. I started wearing miniskirts and heels to school. I was dressing like a black Madonna, but I saw the attention it got me from the guys at school, so the shorter my skirt the better.

When I was a little girl, I used to read encyclopedias, and one day I came across the Declaration of Independence. I was fascinated by the signatures so I would practice them until I got really good at replicating them. Then I learned how to copy signatures, so I would write my excuse letters to get me out of class. My mom had to get a job to bring more income into the house, so she went to work at a restaurant. She hated it so much that she would cry to my stepdad she couldn't work there, because she complained the boss was racist. Me and Ken were skipping school so much, and because we didn't have a phone and my mom was never home to check the mail (I would get it when I got home from school), there was no way for the school to get in touch with her.

We would spend our days at the arcade or roaming the city, barely escaping being kidnapped on several occasions. One time we had to jump out of a moving truck! But anyway, I always managed to keep my grades up, and my brother was failing everything. I let him convince me to hide my report card with him, but we knew that couldn't go on for too long. When half the school year had passed and no report cards, my mom didn't want to hear the school computer was down again, so she decided to go to the school. Man, the worst day of my life. She had to hear about everything all in one day. We got tore up! I was never a snitch when it came to Ken, I just took one for the team.

I was so depressed when we lived in Victorville. I was confused and lost. I felt weird and awkward. My demons always taunted me and although my brother was gone and I wasn't being physically molested, I was still being sexually tormented by Succubus! I would constantly masturbate and I felt dirty and disgusting doing it, but I couldn't stop. On my 13th birthday, for the first time in my life, my mom let me have a few friends over for a small party. That day my head had been spinning and I felt sick to my stomach. And in the middle of my first-ever party with my friends over, I felt a heavy gush, and it felt like my stomach tightened up and then dropped, so I ran to the bathroom and I had started my period. I was prepared for it to start but I wasn't expecting it to be like this.

With the onset of my period, I felt like it was more than just a regular period. It was heavy and draining, and every month when it was that time I turned into a monster. I know that sounds cliché, but my period always started on the full moon. As if I was a werewolf or something. My cramps were overwhelming, I was confused because I wanted to tell someone, anyone about me being molested as a child and that now some demonic spirit was molesting me. I wanted my pain to stop, and mom always had a medicine cabinet full of pills. Maybe if I take a few it will make the pain go away. I opened a bottle and it was full, I figured if I took a couple she wouldn't notice. Perhaps I would just go to sleep and not have to wake up from this nightmare. "Take a few pills!" The voice in my head told me. "Maybe your mom will see you laid out on the floor dying and finally she'll care about you!" I wanted to but just then a louder voice said "Do you really want to die, or do you just want to be seen?" I didn't want to face all these questions, so I just went to bed, knowing I hated my life.

Our financial situation caught up with us and my parents lost their house in Victorville. We always went to Sacramento for the summer but we didn't know then, at that time, this particular summer up North was us being homeless. We thought it was strange that midway Mom came to stay with us though. Now, my aunt and grandmother are the sweetest women you would ever meet in life. My Grand Father, AWESOME!! My uncle, also known as Agent Orange, was the crazy fun Uncle who came to our house every summer and took us either to Disneyland or Magic Mountain without fail. I loved them all very much.

My cousins were spoiled and I think that's why my cousin who smoked weed acted such a fool. She didn't appreciate anything. She was Daddy's little girl, started with good grades, a cheerleader; she was the model daughter. But she got caught up with the wrong crowd. After a while, weed wasn't strong enough for her, and she developed a horrible addiction, to the worst drug, Crack! Her new boyfriend, a PIMP. Literally, was a Pimp, and it didn't take my cousin long to figure out that she needed to make money to pay for her addiction, so she became her boyfriend's main hoe.

My aunt and uncle didn't know that she was taking me to crack houses and leaving me there with pimps and hoes while she ran off to get high. I would sit in a corner scared as hell!!!! While pimps ran in and out of the house, looking at me saying "Whose little girl is this??" "She gone be a bad bitch when she get older". Smiling at me with their gold teeth sparkling. What was I, twelve, thirteen by this time, being exposed to pimps and hoes, left at crack houses. Who would believe that I was seeing this type of shit at this age?

But seeing all this made me not want to smoke weed anymore. My cousin and all the other drug abusers in my family were PSA enough for me. One of my cousins, growing up was absolutely beautiful! She was smart, in college, and one night at a college party cost her, her life! A guy slipped Angel Dust into her drink and she had an episode. He took her to a cemetery and raped her and left her there. After that, she became addicted to drugs, in and out of drug rehab and mental facilities. She would never be the same, and ultimately, she shot herself in the head, right in front of my grandfather. Growing up knowing that story kept me as far away from drugs as I could get.

7. SO IT BEGINS

After a long grueling summer of my mom and Aunt constantly arguing, which is funny because I had never seen my aunt argue with anybody else before, but now she and my mom were going at it, every day. My parents decided it was time for us to get back to Southern Cali, where they had a hotel room all lined up for us. The four of us, my parents, me fourteen, and my sixteen-year-old brother, all living together in a hotel room.

We really didn't get it then, we just thought it was cool that every meal we ate came from a restaurant. I can't remember how long we stayed in the Hotel, but we finally moved into a two-bedroom apartment in San Dimas. Now Ken and I had to share a room. That was torture in itself. My parents were notorious for moving us to the Whitest neighborhoods they could find. I knew it had to do with my mom being robbed in the Seventies in LA at gunpoint. From that moment on, she thought every Black man was a gun-toting thief. That idealism didn't help my brothers any. Makes sense why their punishments would be 30-60 days in their room. Not able to leave out, only for school and bathroom breaks.

Anyway, San Dimas was odd. Lots of white people, but these white people were nice! They weren't racist like the ones in Azusa. It was creepily odd. They would talk to us, and say hi at the grocery store. Blow their horn and wave when we walk down the street. It was like a twisted Mayberry! In my first year of school there, I was a nobody, almost invisible. I made friends with some of the weirdest people. One of my friends was a gay dude who was very awkward, and remember during my time gay people were still in the closet!

Then I ran with the Filipinos, they were cool, but everyone at this school was rich. We lived in an apartment just below the houses on the hill. All my Filipino friends lived in big houses, they dressed nicely, drove Benz and BMWs to school and they always had money. Me, I was a grungy broke little black girl. My brother especially hated San Dimas. He was growing up and coming into his manhood and was trying to figure out who he was and where he fit in. In San Dimas, we discovered that there were a few Black kids who lived in an area that was considered the "ghetto". Just below the train tracks, hahaha!!! Anyway, the little black girls were so silly. They ridiculed my brother, calling him Billy Ocean, because we both have very thick lips, and we had a complex about them, they're teasing annoyed both of us.

Our tradition of cutting school lived on. I had an open period in the school office now and had perfected my mother's signature, so whenever either of us felt we needed to miss class I would write the note, and then when I got to the office, I would pull the note and destroy it, so they could never compare the signature with the real thing. My Mom started working at an elementary school as a computer room teacher, me and my brother both got jobs while still in High School because my mom said we had to help out around the house and that we had to pick a bill to pay.

I worked at Taco Bell and my brother worked at Pizza Hut. I had to pay my mom and pay for my school clothes and whatever else I needed for school while maintaining my grades. Did I mention that I was only fifteen when I started working at Taco Bell? Back then things were much different. A 15-year-old could get a job without a work permit. My parents always gave preferential treatment to me over Ken. They taught me to drive and didn't teach him, they let me drive our little Datsun B210 and he, although older than me, had to sit in the backseat. I always got things from them and they would never buy him anything unless I asked them to buy it for him.

My brother made it through high school with a C average. He had come a long way since elementary. The crazy thing is, he is very smart! After graduation, he went to Citrus Community College and my parents were cool with him being at home as long as he was in school and working, although they still didn't teach him to drive or help him get his driver's license. In fact, I was able to take the car drop him off at work, and then get myself to work. Most times he had to take a bus to work, even though I worked up the street and he worked in Pomona.

He made friends with some of the guys in the San Dimas ghetto, and they were studying Islam at the time. These guys were Militant Nation of Islam, and we, having a history of hatred for white kids, helped my brother fall right into the teachings of Minister Farrakhan. When my mom found out that my brother had a Qur'an in her house she hit the roof. From ignorance comes anger, she told him he better get that shit out of her house, and she freaked out. Then he had always wanted to be a rapper and he submitted a rap to a publishing company that responded to him. She opened his mail and read it, and she cussed him out! She told him that he wasn't shit and ain't gone be shit! My Mom had a real tendency of putting my brother down, and he just took it he had no choice and she made his life a real hell.

Entering into my senior year I had made quite a few friends at San Dimas High. I had a small crew of mostly mixed-black girls that I ran with. We ditched all the time. I had two sets of friends, one set no better than the next. But one set was seniors and the other set was juniors. We were some fast-ass little girls. We started hanging out, going to the Beach, Downtown LA, or Pasadena all during school hours; mind you I always maintained a C average. I always did my homework and passed all my tests. I had a C average because I was never there. If I had gone to class, I would have been an A student.

Two of my friends had a car and because I had the artistry of forgery, I was always invited to ditch with them. I took on a second job at Wendy's so I could afford my senior year activities. But the worst of my behavior started at Taco Bell. Like I mentioned earlier I was fifteen when I started working there. I had a boss who was twenty-seven, he was an Indian guy, but he was in love with me. He quickly promoted me to Crew Leader, and then to Shift Manager by the time I turned 16. He took me to dinner all the time, to Black Angus, Red Lobster, or wherever I told him I wanted to go. He started buying me gifts, clothes, jewelry, and electronics, but we never so much as even held hands.

I was 15 going out on dates with my 27-year-old boss and no one said a word! Not even my parents, you know why? Because they never checked on me and never knew what I was doing. Taco Bell in white San Dimas hired a whole black crew from Pomona. One black guy started working there and he flirted with me all the time. I would work the late shift and when I didn't drive, he would take me home. This made my boss so jealous. He tried to schedule us at different times, but we would come in at off times and hang out just to see each other. Then a new boss came in, she was black also and she brought in her sister, her sister's boyfriend, and his friends. The whole Taco Bell in San Dimas was taken over by black folks!

Because I was made Crew Leader I was given the keys to Taco Bell; now why did they do that? We were a crazy crew! I would lock the store up early, all my friends from school would come in and we would eat the food that was supposed to be thrown away. I got a few of my friend's jobs there. It was always drama at Taco Bell! My boss's sister's boyfriend Jay was always trying to flirt with me on the DL, and his girlfriend knew it. She couldn't stand me, and she was so ghetto. Skinny little black chick with a basket weave, sometimes blue, red, or purple braids in the front.

I didn't like her boyfriend, but he was very aggressively flirting with me. All of us started hanging out after work, drinking until late hours. I would lie to my parents and tell them we had to work late. Then one night I didn't drive and Jay was the only one working that night with a car. He offered to take me home, but he asked me if we could go to the park and talk before going home. Me being so naïve said yes, and he didn't even put the car all the way in park before he started kissing all over me. Now what I have learned over the years is with abuse victims you can go one of two ways, either you will be sexually damaged for life and can't stand sex, or you will turn into a nymphomaniac. Unfortunately, my experience took me towards nympho.

I was still 15 at this time and he was 18. I fought him off me for as long as I could, but after a while, it started to feel good! He was grabbing me and trying to pull my pants off, the normal person would have viewed this as a rape, but for some reason I was enjoying it. He pulled my panties down and straddled me in a position where I couldn't move and then he tried to put it in, but I was technically still a virgin and I screamed so loud. It hurt like HELL! But he was very persistent. He was so big and I don't know if he was really big or if it was because of me being a virgin, but he kept working until he finally got the tip in.

That night, the tip was the best he was gone be able to do, but that one night transformed me. After that, we started having sex all the time. At his house, at the park, in his car. Then he started picking me up from school and I would ditch and go with him wherever. My boss that liked me was so pissed, he told me that everybody knows I'm fucking him and he told me that I was being a "little hoe". It hurt my feelings that he said that knowing how much he liked me, but Jay told me he was saying that because he was jealous that I wasn't fucking him!

Jay's girlfriend had got fired from Taco Bell and wasn't around all the time, but word got back to her about us and she came up to the job ready to fight me! Now I was somewhat of a Tomboy and after fighting my brothers and white kids all my life I really didn't fear anyone, so when she came, I went outside and was not backing down. When she saw I wasn't scared she just talked mess and let everyone break it up. But after that, I wasn't interested in that much drama so I left Jay alone.

Then I started talking to this other guy that I worked with and now I was running off with him every night. I started drinking a lot, getting drunk almost every night, on school nights. Oh, how was I getting alcohol all the time? Well, I had my older sister's ID card, after she got her driver's license, she didn't need her ID anymore so I just took over it. Then all my friends got their hands on fake IDs and we started hitting the clubs on Hollywood Blvd. I never thought of myself as being very pretty because all my friends were mixed, light-skinned girls, and black guys back then liked light-skinned black girls. So, I felt that I had to underdress so I could look cute and get attention. And boy did I get attention!

I started meeting so many guys, and I knew something was wrong with me, I wanted to have sex all the time. I would meet someone in a club, and it went from dancing to kissing on the dance floor then next thing you know we were in the bathroom tearing it up! No protection, no one was teaching me about protection because no one knew what I was doing. I was the wild child when I went out with my friends, I would meet someone and disappear. This turned out to be hazardous for me. I met a guy at the club and he came to San Dimas to pick me up and take me out, but we never ended up going out because he date-raped me, in his car at a park near my home, I was still 16 and he was 21.

But that's what happens when you jump in a man's car wearing a skirt so short your panties are showing. My older sister knew I was using her ID, hell I was clubbing with her when I went to Victorville. We would go out to the base and the guy working the door didn't care that we both walked into the club with the same name on our ID, the base club was full of horny soldiers with very few women, and sometimes they didn't even card me. Again I was sixteen!!! I couldn't go wild when I was with my sister, but we got treated like celebrities when we walked into these clubs. I was having a ball, and about this time any type of control that my mom thought she had was so gone.

8. VIOLATED

I made it through high school, and it was on to college. I went to Citrus with my brother and man, College was crazy. So many guys! Most of my friends from High School went on in separate ways so I made a new crew of friends. I kept up with a few of my old friends, but College friends were into so much more. Class, what class? The student center was popping! Everyone was hanging out, videos were playing on the TV, there was a pool table and video games. We hung out so much, clubbing at night, I was getting dirt drunk, like passing out on tables! Tequila shots, mixed drinks sometimes even beer. I started drinking more if that was even possible. I was drunk every night.

I would come home drunk as hell, and my parents would watch me walk or stumble into the house tore up and wouldn't say a thing. Several guys tried to talk to me at Citrus, but I got boo'd up with this East Coaster. He was hella sexy, he was 19 and he fell in love with me. He wanted to be around me 24/7. It was cute at first, but he was preventing me from talking to all the other guys there. Then he said the words that made me run! He told me he wanted me to be his wife. Please! With all these fine ass dudes running around here. I'm 17, what I look like getting married. He wouldn't stop saying it, so I figured I would make him not like me anymore!

He had a few friends who kept flirting with me, so one night there was a get-together and I was invited but he wasn't. A good friend of his threw this party and I knew my invite was his friend's opportunity to see if

I was as in love with P as he was with me. I failed that test on so many levels. It started with us playing a game of strip Poker, of course, I didn't know how to play Poker, and taking shots. In a room full of all his friends, I removed almost every piece of clothing I had on. I slept with his friend and every attendee at the party couldn't wait to tell P what his girl, whom he was so in love with did that night. He was so hurt! What was wrong with me? Why would I do something like that to him? And you know what? I didn't care! Something was really wrong with me!

Eventually, I was kicked out of school for low-class attendance, I quit Taco Bell and started working at Levitz Furniture. My brother couldn't take my mom anymore so one day when she was at work, he just packed up all his stuff and left. He didn't even tell me that he was leaving. I was hurt and pissed at my mom. I started talking crazy to her because I learned that she was older and tired of giving whippings, so I could say and do what I wanted and she would do nothing about it. And please I was paying bills around this bitch; I dare her to say anything to me! That's how I felt at 17.

I started hanging out late, and she would tell me "If you can't make it home before 1 am I'm locking the door" and she took my key, so I would just stay out until the next day. She couldn't handle me anymore and I think she just gave up trying. One of my friends from High school got back in touch with me and we started hanging out again. We started hanging out with a girl who went to San Dimas High School with us, but I didn't talk to her much at school so I didn't know her that well. She moved in from Pasadena in the middle of my senior year and she was a junior. We had a class together and we talked on occasion, but I had no idea that we were about to get so close.

Mom and stepdad were still taking their Vegas weekend trips, but now they started going on longer vacations, like one- and two-week trips. I was loving life. I always had my friends over when the parents were away. Kay, being from Pasadena knew a lot of guys and one night as we all sat at my house, with my parents away in Vegas thought about what we should do for the night. She suggested that she call her boys, respectively known as the "Party Boys" to come over.

In comes about seven fine-ass black guys from Pasadena and it was a party. My fast ass saw three of them that I liked, but we all got paired up and I ended up with DJ. He wasn't my first choice, but he worked. These guys were a little different than what I had previously dealt with. They were all considered the "hoes" of their high school. They were all athletes and all very sexually active. Within a matter of minutes, we got into the hot tub at my house to talk and I think maybe three words were said to each other before DJ started going down on me under the water.

We all started drinking and next thing you know we were in my mom's bed. I didn't realize it but none of my other friends was doing what I was doing. They were all over the place, but just chilling. So, when the other guys saw that I was giving it up, they all got real interested in me. Of course, when the night was over and the next day came, DJ wasn't calling me and trying to get to know me or develop a relationship! I was just a fuck. Soon this became a ritual, and I wasn't just sleeping with him. DJ passed my number to his friends and I was getting calls from a few of the Party boys, except one. He was dating Kay and he knew I wouldn't do anything with him because of that.

One night all the guys were chilling at one of the boys' houses, so me and two of my friends went to hang out with them. DJ got me upstairs into one of the rooms and we started having sex. I had been drinking, of course, the room was dark, but I could see the door open and then close. I asked him who was in the room, and he said no one so we went back to what we were doing. Then the door opened and closed a few more times, I tried to sit up but before I knew it Kay's boyfriend had put his hand over my mouth and told me if you scream, I'll punch you in the face. I laid down and DJ got off me and someone else got on me. Then he got off and someone else got on! I couldn't believe they were raping me. It was about six guys in there. Kay's man was telling me to stop crying and that they were doing this because they all liked me, telling me how sexy I was and that they couldn't resist me. I guess this was supposed to make me feel good about being raped. He was the last to get on. He started kissing me and telling me how much he liked me, but by this time I was numb. I couldn't hear anything or feel anything.

When he got off me, I got up and ran to a bathroom that was

attached to the room and locked myself in. I didn't know that my friends had left me because they thought I was upstairs being a willing participant to this. So, I'm in the house, locked in the bathroom with all my friends gone. The guys started to get scared because they thought I was going to call the police. DJ sat at the door begging me to let him in the bathroom. I could hear the guys outside the door, saying "What if she calls the police? I can't get in trouble!" So, I stayed in the bathroom. I got up, walked over to the sink, and looked at myself in the mirror. My head started spinning. I looked over and saw the medicine cabinet. I opened it and there were a few pill bottles in it.

I picked one up and read it a little, opened it up, and looked inside. That voice in my head said "Just take the pills. It won't matter if you die, no one cares anyway!" It kept saying it and it kept getting louder and louder until I finally put a few pills in my hand and just popped them in my mouth, but the second I did the louder voice yelled "SPIT IT OUT!" And I did just that, right into the toilet. I sat on the floor and cried and then after a while I let DJ in and he tried to convince me that he didn't know they were in the room and they did that to me. Then Kay's man came in the bathroom, the other guys had left. I had to get home so we started talking, and he apologized. Now you would think that this should have traumatized me, but it didn't.

First thing the next day Kay and my other friend came over to the house. I didn't know that she wanted to fight me because she thought I was upstairs just giving it up to everybody like a buffet, but when I told her what happened, she calmed down. I don't think she all the way believed me, but we were cool after that. But then Stockholm Syndrome kicked in, the guys kept calling me, picking me up, taking me out, and the funny thing is I was not scared of them. The worst that could happen to me already happened so I was just like whatever!

Well, soon all their friends knew and I started meeting all these guys from Pasadena and I turned into a sex feign. I don't even know how many different guys I was having sex with, maybe eight or nine. I had a different guy picking me up every night of the week and my mom never asked to meet anyone, she just watched the buzzer for the door go off and saw me dash out with a quickness. My battle with suicide was deeper than I had ever led on to anyone. I always felt like I was spiraling out of control. A hue of redness would come over me and I would warp in my mind to a different state of consciousness.

I would feel like I was sleep-walking sometimes, straight to the bathroom, to the medicine cabinet and I would usually wake up with a bottle of pills in my hand. Just to show you how much no one paid attention to me, in San Dimas our apartment had one bathroom, so when I would wake up, I would be standing in a daze staring in the mirror, with a bottle of pills in my hand and it went completely unnoticed! Until the night I actually swallowed some pills! I just remember getting up to use the bathroom, I would walk past the medicine cabinet and unconsciously pick up the pills, but most nights I would wake up before taking them. On this particular night, the pills made it into my mouth. I went back to my bed to lie down and I started spinning. I jumped up and ran to the bathroom because I thought I was going to throw up, but before I did, I blacked out, and I woke up in the hospital. I don't even know what the doctor told my parents, but I went home after a few hours, and then life continued as if nothing ever happened!

9. WILD CHILD

Me and my girls were clubbing like crazy. One of my friends was funny, we would go out to a club and if she wasn't having fun she would just get up and leave, the one who left me the night the guys raped me, and she was always the one driving. One night she left me at a club in Hollywood, I was inside dancing, I came out and she was nowhere to be found. I had met this guy who said he was Al B. Sure's drummer and he asked me if I wanted to go to an after-party with all the celebrities. I was down, but when we got there, it was wild, even for me!

Just naked girls running all over the place, sucking on dudes in all corners, and cocaine on the tables just freely out in the open. Drugs are not my thing so I didn't want to stay long. I told him I lived in San Dimas, and that I had to be home soon. We left and he jumped on the freeway, but going the total opposite direction of San Dimas, he headed back towards Inglewood. Just as my fears told me, he took me to his home in Ladera Heights. He had a beautiful house with windows everywhere and a large piano in the middle of the living room.

He kept talking about him being Al B.'s drummer, whatever. I didn't want to hear about all this I just wanted to go home. Then out of nowhere, he told me I had to strip for him if I wanted to get a ride home. I was pissed; I just wanted to get home. Then he took out a gun and put it on the dresser and told me to take my fucken clothes off. Now I was petrified, but I figured I better just do this willingly, what other way was this going to end up? I gave him the best strip show that I knew how to give. When all my clothes

44

were off, he grabbed me by my arm, threw me on the bed, smashed my face on the pillow and he grabbed my hair so tight and started fucking me from behind. He kept asking me if I wanted it in my ass and I was begging him not to. I had never done that and it was a scary thought.

Luckily, he didn't, after he finished, I curled up in a ball on the bed and he got up, got dressed, and left! I had no idea where he went or where I was. I put my clothes on and went out the front door but I was in an all-residential neighborhood. I went back in the house and figured damn he already raped me what more can happen; well, he could come in with a bunch of guys and let them all take turns raping me. I don't know, all I could do was just wait for his ass to get back and hopefully, he will take me home. The sun came up and he finally came back. He acted like nothing ever happened and said let's go. It was a quiet ride home but thank God, he took me home, and lucky for me this was a weekend that my parents were gone. I went into the house, took a shower, fell onto my bed, and cried myself to sleep. What was happening to me? Why was I being raped on so many different occasions? I had been date raped twice, gang raped, and now this! I had no one I could tell any of this to, so I kept it bottled up inside.

About four months after being raped twice in a short period of time, I woke up one morning and I felt something fluttering around in my stomach. I was still having my period, although it was much shorter than usual! Rather than the usual 7-8 days it was only lasting 2-3 days and it was very light. Am I pregnant? Naw couldn't be. Time passed and yep, you guessed it I was pregnant. But I couldn't tell anyone. So, I started working out, tying up my stomach and wearing large baggy clothes.

Kay was the only person I told. We still went out, we still partied, I kept drinking, still having sex with multiple partners, and for the first four months I was having a period until one day it stopped. As time went on, I really started feeling the baby move inside of me, that was confirmation. Kay had introduced me to another friend of hers that was pregnant Tray, but I didn't tell her that I was pregnant. She was with her baby's daddy and she was all excited about her pregnancy, having baby showers, all cute and fat. We started talking on the phone a lot and we got close as friends. I wanted to tell her, but I figured I will in time.

One day I was sitting in the house and there was a knock on the door. I went downstairs and my mom opened the door, it was Ken! He was walking on a cane and his head had stitches everywhere. During the time he was gone, me and my older sis had been all over LA looking for him, and we had found out that he went from being homeless to living in an F.O.I. house. The Fruit Of Islam, it's a house where they teach young black boys how to become men.

Well, he and some of the guys had been out jogging one morning and the police stopped them and demanded to see their ID. Of course, they were out jogging and didn't have ID on them, so the police commanded them to sit on the curb and they refused because they were being harassed. The police called for backup and then it turned into a standoff between them and the police. I wasn't there so I don't know all the details, but Billy clubs were flying and they all started fighting. My brother was fighting the police, and they rat-packed him and started hitting him in the head, legs, and the side of his body. They basically were going for blood and didn't care if they killed him or not. They left him for dead, in fact when the ambulance came for him, he said he could hear them saying they lost one. He mustered enough energy to move his finger and they were able to save him. He was taken to the hospital and as soon as he was well enough to go to jail, they threw him in a cell, stitches in his head and all. When he got out, he came home.

I sat there in tears listening to his story, then we went upstairs and he told me of his last few years of being homeless and living on the streets and in the library. I had to be about five months pregnant at this time, I told him to feel my stomach and he felt the baby move. He jumped out of his skin, and he said "Oooooh you in trouble", but I shushed him and told him not to tell.

My other sis had been away in the military and was finally back in California. She was so excited to come to the house and announce to my parents that she was pregnant by her boyfriend. I don't think she ever had any intentions of being with this guy, but she was having a baby. She came in and told us, but she kept looking at me funny. She pulled me into the kitchen and asked me "Are you pregnant?" I quickly told her no, but I knew that my time was short and I wasn't going to be able to hide it much longer. I knew the time had come and that I was going to be showing soon, so one night I told my mom that I needed to talk to her. I sat there shaking and I just said it, "I think I'm pregnant", and all she said was "I know! We better call the doctor tomorrow!" That was it, that's all she said to me. I was nineteen now and I was working, so she didn't trip out too much.

We went to the doctor and found out that I was seven months pregnant!!! Then I thought about all the things I had been doing, the drinking, the crazy sex parties, the clubbing. I got really worried; I hoped I hadn't done anything to the baby. I stopped going out and drinking, I thought I better start preparing for the birth of this child. Luckily a year prior, I had a car accident and now a year later I received a settlement of twenty thousand dollars that came about the time of me announcing my pregnancy.

That money should have made a difference in my life but honestly, my parents juiced me for a lot of the money, then we ate and shopped the rest of the money away. I kept asking my mom to take me to buy a car, but she told me not to waste my money on a car. Boy was I a fool! So, I went baby shopping, buying the most expensive baby stuff I could find. I was ready for this, or maybe I wasn't! Only one month had passed from the time that I had announced that I was pregnant, but suddenly I started to get really sick.

I was dizzy all the time and my feet had swelled to an enormous size. I went to my regular doctor's appointment and the doctor looked at me, took my blood pressure, and told me at that time, we have to get this baby out of you today! She told me that I had pre-eclampsia, (gestational high blood pressure), and if she didn't induce my labor, I could have a seizure. So, I was rushed to the hospital that day and my labor was induced. After getting oxytocin it only took three hours for the baby to come. They gave me Demerol but it still hurt like all hell!

I learned two important things about myself when I went to the hospital to give birth. The first is I have a very rare blood type and I had to have an injection to prevent my body from attacking the baby. I thought it was strange that my blood type was what they consider an "Alien" blood type! Second, I can't handle any drug of any type. Taking drugs is not safe for me because of the attack that I am under spiritually. I feel like any portal that opens up for me is a gateway.

After I gave birth, as I was in the hospital room, I sat up in the bed. The hospital was eerily quiet, so I got out of my bed to find a nurse so they could bring the baby to me, I was so drugged up I hadn't seen her yet. As I approached the nurse's station there was no one there. No nurses, no doctors, no one. I saw bodies lying in the beds in the room so I walked down the hall a little further. I turned the corner and on the floor were white bunnies, just hoping all around. It creeped me out so I went back to my room and sat up in the bed and pulled the blanket up to my chest. Just then an old white man walked into my room and sat on my bed. He asked me "Can you see me?" "Yes, I can see you" I replied. Then he said "Wow! Remarkable!" and he stood up and walked out of the room. This didn't feel like a dream.

On May 26th I had an even five-pound beautiful, little baby girl. I was watching "Who's the Boss" and saw the name Alyssa Milano and it was settled, Alysa Brianna. She had to stay in the hospital for a little over a week because her birth weight dropped and she was jaundiced. But I finally brought her home and I was finally in love. I was excited to have a baby because honestly, I didn't feel loved by anyone.

I felt like my parents saw me running crazy and didn't give a fuck. And I was having all this sex with no emotions, a baby is just what I needed so I could cuddle her and see what love feels like. HA! This baby cried day and night! She had colic and she would not shut up. My Mom said you had her you take care of her. So, here we are, me and Alysa, her lying on the bed screaming her lungs out, me sitting on the edge of the bed crying my eyes out. Around the time she was three months old, the curiosity of "Who's the father" arose. So, the guys couldn't wait to get a glimpse of her and try to compare her look, but it was no doubt, hands down DJ's baby! She looked just like him, Whew! That's what I had told everyone and I prayed hard on it.

10. BABY MAKES TWO

Alysa was an amazing baby! She was incredibly smart. She was so alert and I could tell that she knew what was going on around her. She was my little "road dog". Unfortunately, she didn't stop me from partying. We did a lot of house parties and poor Alysa would be right in the middle of our parties. Sometimes I would be passed out drunk and my baby would be lying next to me screaming her head off and someone would come and get her for me and take care of her until I came to. My Mom wouldn't watch her at first, but as she got older, she and my mom bonded and my mom started watching her for me. Me and Kay started to hit the Hollywood club scene. We went to the club almost every night, then she decided that we should get into the entertainment industry and start up a girl's group. Her dad had written a few scripts for some popular TV shows back in the day and he told us we could be singers if we focused and practiced.

So, she had a cousin who knew people and next thing you know he was hyping us up. We started doing a whole lot of nothing with him. He was married with a son and we constantly hung out at their house, trying to put some music together. He was a Muslim, but he came on to me hard and next thing you know we started having sex. He was twenty-eight; his history was ex-pimp, a drug dealer turned Muslim now looking to get into the entertainment industry. He was very experienced sexually; he did things to me that were beyond my realm of sexual experiences.

He didn't just have sex, he made it a whole erotic experience. He taught me how to properly give "head", such as focusing on certain veins on the penis, working the tip, and using your teeth the right way so as not to bite it but to slightly scrape it with the teeth. Ice in the mouth, not being afraid of a man cumming in your mouth and swallowing. Because of my history of sexual abuse, I was not uncomfortable with having a (excuse the word) dick in my mouth, I know the context sounds disturbing, but it is what it is. It was as if he was schooling me to be a prostitute. I know that wasn't his intent, he just wanted me to take care of him and do the things that he likes, but it was so intense. He used to tell me "You're a natural" and told me I was a "pro" and how did I learn so fast, that it seemed as if I already knew what I was doing. Pimps play mind games with their words, and because I was a young girl I fell for all of it, he blew my mind. I was so addicted to him. Then he booked a show for us, it was a talent show in Santa Maria, a town right next to Santa Barbara and Lompoc. We put a song together, and Kay's brother put a dance step together for us. We had the outfits, we had the look, but did we have the talent?

Believe it or not that night our competition was a, not known then, but now very famous J. Foxx. He was new in the industry and had just arrived in California from Texas. He did a comedy act and his friend Speedy performed as well. The crowd liked us. They went crazy with the applause, but he and his friend were funnier than our singing was entertaining. He won first, Speedy came in second and we came in third. That was a victory to me, but Kay's cousin went off. He said we weren't serious and that he was wasting his time with us. Just like that our group was over. He stopped calling me and stopped coming to get me. He cut off everything, the sex, the music. I was upset and it threw me into a slight depression. I wanted to hurt myself but I didn't want it to hurt. So, I just drank, a lot. I started drinking Cisco's and gin.

Kay liked J and in Santa Maria and they had exchanged numbers. But the night of the talent show she asked me to go tell him that she wanted to talk to him, but when I went over to tell him, he said "Well I like you" and he started singing in my ear, and he gave me his number but I didn't call him. He started doing performances at various clubs in LA and I kept seeing him out. One night I saw him, and he asked me to meet him in the back of the club in the dressing room. One thing led to another and he bent me over, lift up my skirt, and fucked the shit out of me!

After that every time I saw him, my skirt was lifted and my panties were on the floor. I think one night in my drunken stupor, I went back and told Kay that he liked me and she and I got into the biggest fight. She told me that I had a problem and I knew she was right, I did have a problem! A problem that no one would ever understand. She told me she didn't want to be my friend anymore and I was completely crushed. Our friendship ended that night and that ruined me. I loved her as a friend and I didn't want to do anything to hurt her, but I did with my destructive behavior. I felt out of control at this point, I had a serious problem and I didn't know what to do about it. I couldn't talk to anyone because what would I say? I have a spirit that's molesting me and causing me to have uncontrolled sexual behavior.

My nightmares worsened! I was still having the dream but now I started having dreams that I was in a bubble and the bubble was closing in on me and I couldn't breathe, I felt like I was choking. Then I had a recurring dream that a large snake was chasing me and I was running as fast as I could, but he would slap me with his tail and I would fall to the ground and he would wrap his body around me and squeeze me until I felt like I was going to explode. The other dream I had was me looking into the window of our old house in Azusa and I could see my whole family, and when we turned around everyone was covered in blood and we looked demonic. That dream scared me so much. Then I kept dreaming that I would be running from a group of guys who obviously wanted to rape me, but while running I would take off into flight and they would look up at me in astonishment as I flew through the sky.

But the one that scared me the most and it was the most recurring, was the beast. He became a black shadow that stood over me no matter where I was. On the swings, and in my room, in my sleep he would keep me locked up in the dark chamber, still handcuffed to the chair while he sexually used me. I started having sleep paralysis. I would try to scream in my sleep to wake myself up, but nothing would come out. I would hear the pulsating of my heart getting louder and louder, feeling like he was trying to take my breath! Then I would cry out to God and I would instantly wake up! My dreams were stressing me out. My dreams were describing my feelings, but I didn't get it at the time. I just wanted to die, but I couldn't feel that way, who would take care of Alysa? I quit my job, got on welfare sat in the house, and wouldn't leave.

After a while, my mom got tired of me sitting around the house and she started complaining about every little thing. She didn't see my depression! She never saw me; she would just cover everything up by taking me out to eat. I was drowning, so I decided at age twenty that I needed to get away! I went on a search to find my biological Dad and I remembered where his cousin lived so I went to LA and found him. I asked him if me and Alysa could come to stay with him. While I was there, I went out every night and left Alysa for him and his wife to watch her. After a week he came to me and asked me if I was ready to go home. I was like "I can't go home, I ran away", but he told me that his wife said I couldn't stay, that I was too wild! Can you imagine that? So, I had to bite my lip and go home. I had him take me home and on the ride home I asked him if he ever abused my mom and my sisters. He told me "No baby, I loved my family and I would never do anything to hurt any of you!" It just felt like a lie. It was Mother's Day, all my siblings were at the house, and I just walked in the door and went to my room like nothing ever happened. My Mom didn't say a word to me; she just gave me the evil eye.

11. A NEW DARKNESS

So starts a new chapter in my life. After Kay ended our friendship Tray became my new party buddy. She had left her son's father and had an apartment in Highland, CA. so Alysa and I moved in with her and her son. Tray had an incredible Mom, and she took me and Alysa in as her own, she was the loving Mother I never had. Her stepfather was a fan of Malcolm X and whenever I would go to their house, he would have conversations with me about being black. Ken had become a very militant Muslim and I stopped eating pork a few years back because he would come into the house and go off on me if he saw me eating it. My mom got mad at me because I stopped eating it, but Tray's stepdad didn't eat pork and when I would come over, they would cook only chicken and turkey, especially for me! I felt like this was the family I was supposed to be born into!

Tray was always my most level-headed friend. She is very intelligent and always made clear concise decisions even as a young girl. She started working for the State at a young age and she was a bit of a square, she was just what I needed in my life. She had only dated one guy who she had her son by, but I was getting ready to change all that. She and I started to party a lot. I dressed very risqué and now I had her dressing like me! We went to LA every weekend and stayed with her step-sister when we were out there. We rolled with the Escort car club on Crenshaw by day and we hit up every Hollywood club at night, we became regulars. We danced with all the entertainers and got into the VIP section at the clubs. Everybody knew us and I thought I was the finest thing on two legs. If I saw a guy in the club that I wanted, I got him.

I met the finest guy who fell in love with me and asked me to marry him but I was too wild for marriage. I would talk to everybody, exchange numbers with every fine guy in the club, and hook up with all of them. They would drive all the way to Highland to come see me, about sixty miles away from LA. I was still being reckless sexually, but I had to be more discrete, I didn't want Tray to see that side of me. She actually calmed me down a little bit. But after a while, she met a new guy and fell in love and that was the end of my party buddy!

Me and Alysa had to move out, and my mom wasn't having me back so easily so I made the worst mistake ever. I moved in with my older brother! Yes, the brother that molested me. I finally got the nerve to tell my mom about him molesting me as a child and she told me, "That's something we should never discuss with anyone. But you have to be a good Christian and forgive him!" So, I thought I was supposed to just forgive and forget!

He had been in the Military and met a girl, got married, and had two kids. I thought he shaped up because when they split, he took the kids with him so I agreed to move in to help him with them. He had got kicked out of the Military because he had a drinking problem and I was getting ready to find out how severe it was. I was still leery of him and he having a young daughter in the house made me even more nervous, so I made her stick by my side. But he was too much, he was drunk all the time, he woke up and blasted The Ghetto Boys and Ice Cube, which I didn't mind the music but the lyrics were nothing but cussing and I tried to tell him with kids in the house we shouldn't be playing that type of music, but he would cuss me out royally in front of the kids. This arraignment couldn't last long, and I would find out the hard way.

We had the family over for Thanksgiving and he cussed me out in front of our Minister Uncle and my elderly grandmother, and then kicked everybody out of the house, including me and Alysa. I packed my stuff and left with my sister. I hated to leave my niece with him, but luckily, soon after I left the kids went back to live with their mother. I went back to Victorville to live with my older sis and her crazy husband. And crazy he was!

A lot of this is going to sound strange but it is all true. Her husband had a very weird aura about him, and from the time my sister had got with him a lot of strange things had been going on around her. Her daughter is a year older than Alysa and she was born a medium, she was born in her sac. I say this because she used to wake up in the middle of the night, sit at the foot of the bed, and watch us sleep, and when me and my sister woke up the curtains flew up and you could feel a gush of wind in the room even though the windows were closed, yeah just like in the movie Poltergeist. Furniture would move and doors would slam!

I always thought her husband had a bad energy of his own and felt like he transferred what energy he had to me and my sister, so now I had a second entity within me. This one was very unfamiliar, because odd to say my dark energy had been with me all my life and I knew it was only sexually assaulting me. This one, I had no idea of its intentions. I felt he sent it out of anger because when I moved in, we started going out, and this was because my sister wanted to go out, but he thought it was my doing. My sister moved into a house and this house also had bad energy in it. In my sleep, I could hear footsteps all around the house and I could hear the walls breathing. Something would sit on the bed and you could see the imprint of where it was sitting. I don't know if the house had its own bad energy or if her husbands had followed us! I was ready to go home, so I had to call my mom and beg her to let me come home. She said yes and I knew I had to act right in order to stay. I had moved too many times in a short period of time, and all this was no good for Alysa.

12. STREETLIFE

My Military sis had met a guy and they had been planning to get married. But one minute they were getting married, the next minute they weren't. After I talked to them and convinced them to do it, the wedding was on. I had to convince them because we had already paid for the reception. I had been talking to Ken and he told me he was coming for the wedding, but he told me about a friend of his named MM and they were doing some stuff to make money. So, I started talking to his friend on the phone and it was all business. I knew he was playing the conversation safe because he didn't know what I looked like. Ironically, I discovered that I had met him before while working at Taco Bell. He came in one night acting like a pimp and asked me for my number, but I think he scared me and I didn't give it to him, can't remember all the details.

So anyway, Ken showed up to the wedding in a new Black Nissan Maxima and he told us it was rented. After the wedding, my sis and her new husband were going to Vegas and they invited me and Ken to come. Ken had money, and he was paying for everything so I asked him "What's up" what are you doing? How do you have all this money? He laughed and told me the car was stolen. He had us rolling to Vegas in a stolen car and he didn't even bother to tell any of us. When we got back from Vegas, I told him I was going to LA with him. He didn't want me to go with him but I had to get out of my mom's house. I told him if I stayed there, I was going to commit suicide and that was no joke. I literally had to battle this damn voice in my head, every day telling me that my life was worthless and that I needed to end it. I told him that I cried each night as I struggled with this voice. So, we left with him and went to LA. I didn't know my brother was sleeping in his car! Now me and Alysa was sleeping in the car with him. Some nights we slept at his friend's studio, but we were officially homeless. I knew he was into some illegal stuff, but I had no idea what he was into. He told me MM was in the check game and to come up all you needed was a bank account, and my BofA account was ready to be used.

The first time I laid eyes on MM I was in love! We met him in an alley in Pasadena. He pulled up in his convertible Mustang 5.0, bouncing around with the most beautiful smile I had ever seen on a man. He came over to me and said "Ken, this your sister??? "Man, you didn't tell me your sister was so fine", all I could do was blush. Then he saw Alysa, and he said "Awwww, look at the baby" That was all I needed to hear. This had to be my future husband. He told me "Let's go talk!" I asked Ken to watch Alysa so we could go talk "business".

I got in the Mustang with him and he threw a sack on my lap and asked me to count the money inside it. Twenty bands, then he told me to put it in the glove compartment. I opened the glove box and there was a gun, I didn't care. I was ready to be about that life! We got a hotel room and on day one, just meeting him, he and I made love. It wasn't just sex, it felt different from all the other guys I had been with, we connected, and after attending the ex-pimp school of sex, I blew his mind with my head game. He was hooked just as bad as me. I felt it was all too good to be true! And it was. I soon found out that he was in a relationship. He was living with the mother of his daughter and I met her but I didn't care. I knew for sure that I was going to be able to get him and make him forget all about her.

A few days later we deposited a check into my bank account for fifty thousand dollars. He told me we had to wait a few days before I could pull the money, then on the first day of withdrawal I pulled out thirty thousand in cashier checks, and since everything was going so well, why not deposit another check for twenty thousand? The next few days were just going to the bank and pulling out money. When it was over, before the bank realized that we were using stolen checks, I had pulled out over sixty thousand dollars. I paid the big boys their cut and my cut was a little over thirty thousand dollars, cash in my hand.

Me and Ken went crazy. I put us both into our own spots, I got a penthouse in the Wilshire District and put Ken around the corner from me. MM came to the crib with a briefcase, pulled out a laptop and he had a little machine that looked like a card reader! He had a stack of credit cards and a stack of papers that had the info of unlimited high-credit customers. Right in the middle of the living room, he made me and Ken some cards to use but the stripe on the back didn't match the number on the front, so it was very risky using them. I didn't care, I jumped into the game with both feet first. I got a little job working at an Art Gallery in Pasadena as a front and put Alysa in Marcus Garvey, a highly accredited academic school in LA. Me and Ken ran around like two big-ass kids! Buying whatever we wanted. Computers, Big Screen TVs, Clothes, shoes, jewelry, video games, water guns lol! I was out in them LA streets running wild! I was driving around town like a mad woman. Getting in fights in the middle of the street. Having guns pulled on me. Crashing into cars to get away! Then the LA riots broke out. We were looting and protesting in the streets. I was unhinged, totally reckless!

MM and I had a wild sex life. We had sex everywhere; it didn't matter where we were and who was around. If we was horny we was fucking. One day he came over to my house and he had someone with him, he said it was his cousin, you know how they play that brother/cousin game. But right in front of his cousin he started kissing me and laid me down on the bed and we started going at it. It felt weird with his boy right there watching us but I kind of knew where this was heading. He told me he wanted to make his cousin jealous and see what kind of pussy he was getting. He told me "Come on baby, give him some head while you fuck me" I really didn't want to, and was a little apprehensive, so I said no at first.

He got mad that I told him I didn't want to, then he kind of flipped on me and said, "shit, if you don't I know some other bitches that will". Damn do we have to go here, fine I thought, I'll do it if it's that serious. Then he said let my cousin fuck, and like a fool, I did. After we finished, he said "I can't believe you fucked on my cousin like that!" I was so confused, you told me to! Head games. This opened up a whole new door for MM and me. The next time it was two more of his friends, and then it got up to parties with a lot of dudes. Hard to say this, but this life was better than the life I was currently living, so I rolled with it.

At least I was making money, we were drinking Dom Perigon, eating at the best Restaurants in LA, and constantly shopping. He used me as an entertainment piece. I would just get drunk and next thing you know I was fucking on a room full of niggas. I was in denial about this part of my life for so long. I had to move like a stealth rocket not to be exposed. The only stupid part of this whole thing is that he wasn't putting the money directly in my pocket for doing it. I was dressed like a million bucks! Hair and nails stayed fresh but where was the cash? I was being pimped and I didn't like that.

So, I started finding customers on my own so I could get paid off my skills. It was a very dangerous game I was playing because MM was a psycho! He would grab me by the neck and tell me if he found out I was fucking around he would put me in the dirt, and then he would laugh like he was joking. If we were out and another guy looked at me even in the car, he would literally in traffic, pull the car over pop the glove box, grab the heater, and walk up to a niggas window and be like "You like what you see Patna! You looking at my girl? What the fuck you tryin' to do! Oh, you think you can take her? Yeah nigga, that's what the fuck I thought!" And then skip back to the car laughing. Crazy. I was too deep in and there was nowhere else to go from here! The money was good, and at least now I was getting paid to fuck rather than niggas taking it from me!

I started venturing into other crimes, like stealing cars! I became a professional car thief and developed a name for myself around LA. People were telling Ken, I heard about your sister, they were calling me and MM, Bonnie, and Clyde. I would go out with a crew of guys and we were strapped with wire cutters and tools. The guys would be scared as hell, shaking and sweating, I would walk up to them and be like "You alright? If you can't handle this shit take yo ass home" like I was some hard ass! We would break the lock box off the window of the new cars, get the keys, jump into the car, and drive off like it was nobody's business, straight to our chop shop connect.

MM was mad at me for stealing cars and didn't like the crew of people we had around us, but he was venturing into other mess himself. I knew someone was controlling all this that was bigger than MM, and my snooping paid off! I found out it was an older woman. I had to meet her! I begged and pleaded with him to introduce me to her, and I finally met her. She pulled up in her white Jag, with her black shades on and a scarf around her head. She looked like straight money, but she was on the phone, we all had cell phones back then, not just pagers. But she was cussing someone out so bad. Her mouth was the worst "Look muthafucka, if you ain't got my fucken money we running up in that bitch, guns cocked ready to blow yo fucken head off!" DANG! Then she got off the phone and in the sweetest motherly voice she said: "MM is this your new girl"? "She's so cute" and of course, she fell in love with Alysa, she was such a charming baby. After that meeting me and Ma became inseparable. Aside from committing crime she always had a project she was working on.

Ken, MM, Ma, and all the people I was around were Muslims and I started going to the Nation of Islam, Mosque in LA. It was a weird feeling because I was not knowing and I would go to the Mosque with short dresses on or tight low-cut tops, you know dresses for church and of course, instead of leading me right, all the women in the mosque snubbed their noses at me. I didn't feel comfortable going to the Mosque but I loved to listen to Minister Farrakhan speak and I loved the teachings of Islam.

I was Ma's daughter she never had. She had one son and he was a spoiled rotten little f-up! Ma and I started shopping, going to lunch, and hanging out. Then she realized that I could duplicate any signature that I saw, so we started getting checks together, like taking them from attorney's offices or auto mechanic shops and I would dup the sig on them and had the crew roll them.

We were the perfect duo, I was shopping at stores in Beverly Hills, on Sunset, and on Rodeo Dr. She had her tailor-made clothes designed especially for me and Alysa had a wardrobe fit for a celebrity baby. We shopped with stolen credit cards, and we started to get too comfortable with them. I drove around the streets of LA looking like a celebrity in my little drop-top Benz! One day a police officer pulled me over and my heart stopped because the car I was in was stolen. This LAPD officer walks up to my car and said "Miss the reason I pulled you over was to get your name and number, because you are too damn fine!" I think I gave him my correct number out of shock, so he called me and invited me to a pool party! It was a whole police party and it was worse than the celebrity parties I had been to! I kid you not!

These police were using drugs, they had naked girls running around and this fine but ridiculously strong-ass police officer damn near raped me! I told him I had to use the bathroom and I ran up out of there so fast! This was my life.

Anyway, MM had friends and family in the mid-west, and what happened there was the start of the worst part of my life. He sent me to the mid-west to do some shopping for them with the credit cards. I got there and we went to this expensive furniture store and I bought them thousands of dollars worth of furniture, like $30k worth. Then we got stupid. I went into the mall to buy some shoes, and the lady at the counter swiped the credit card, she looked at the receipt and the card and noticed that the numbers didn't match. She started yelling for security and I took off running, the security guard caught me and I was arrested!

Wait was I going to jail? This wasn't supposed to happen! I get to this little hick jail in Kansas and within a few hours, MM's friends had bailed me out! I was so ready to go home at this point. But that's not what happened! He told his friends that I would entertain them while I was there. I didn't know anything about that part, but after being arrested I just wanted to get out of the mid-west, but nope I was held hostage literally for a week in a house of men I didn't know, and I was there to be their little sexual entertainment piece. At least they paid me, that was the only part that made it worth it. And then one of the guys fell in love with me! Ugghhh. And MM had the nerve to get mad at me about that!

When I finally got home Ma was fixing up a school and she needed power tools, so we went to a tool rental place and used a credit card. Everything went through but she never returned the tools, so the place found out that we had used a stolen card, and an alert was put on us. Then

MM told me that he had an inside connect for a cash advance at some check cashing place, where all I had to do was go in and give the girl the card and she would give me the cash off the credit card.

Well, the girl behind the counter was sleeping with him and of course, I didn't know that part, so when she saw me, she got mad and let her manager call the police on me. I ran out of there, got into my stolen car, and drove off. Soon I had a police car behind me. The police got on his loudspeaker and said "Driver pull over!" where was I going, I pulled over. The Police jumped out of his car on full adrenaline, with his gun drawn, I was thinking "What the hell, is that a gun pointed at my head!" He started screaming "GET DOWN ON THE GROUND" and in my head, I said "I can't get on the ground in this outfit", but when you have a gun pointed at your head you just jump your ass on the ground. He pulled out his handcuffs and pulled my arm to my back and then my other arm. He had both my arms and a handful of my hair, that's how far up he had my hands.

I started crying and telling him that he was hurting me and he screamed "SHUT YOUR MOUTH!" He locked the handcuffs so tight on my hands I could feel the handcuffs cutting my wrist. He picked me up by the handcuffs and threw me in the back of the police car! OK, this was bad. I was scared! He took me to the Northridge jail and put me in a cell full of prostitutes. They all looked at me and was like "Awww baby are you ok?", "you look like a kid" Then they all started talking to me and made me feel comfortable. I met a girl who knew my cousin from up North, they had worked the streets together. By that night MM had come and bailed me out. I never wanted to go to jail again. That was the worst experience ever! But did I stop criming? Nope, something was wrong with me, that should have scared me straight, so Ma and MM told me not to do anything else, but I think Ma forgot she said that.

It was back to school time and Ma always liked to be the one buying a bunch of stuff for her nieces and nephews, so she decided she was going to get everybody Nikes. Each pair was about a hundred dollars or more, and she had about fifteen pairs. She gave me a credit card and told me to go to the counter to pay, and what do you know the stupid lady behind the counter looks at the credit card. I snatched the credit card from her hand, but she snatched it back quicker! I took off running. I ran out of the mall parking lot, across a busy street, and into a residential neighborhood.

I saw a camper shell in someone's yard and figured that was the best place to hide. Just my luck, it was the yard of an off-duty police officer. Go fucking figure! When he saw the police looking for me, he showed them exactly where I was. I was handcuffed again and off to jail. They arrested Ma at the store. The other times that I had been arrested Alysa was with Ken, but this time I had moved in with some friends and my friend Bea was watching Alysa. I figured I would go to jail overnight and be out the next day. Not this time, everything had caught up with me and I couldn't get bail!

During the time I was arrested, Ken went to steal a car and got caught, so now he was in jail too. We both got arrested at the same damn time! A few days had passed, and I had to get Alysa somewhere safe because my friend's husband had left a loaded gun on the bed and my two-year-old baby picked up the gun and shot it through the window. I had to call my older sister; she was the only one I could tell this to. She immediately ran to LA and got Alysa, and she instantly told my mom that I was in jail.

13. PRISON BOUND

I was taken to Sybil Brand jail in LA. It was a nightmare, one of the worst women's jails in the country. I was put in a dorm with 250 women. Everything was cold metal and concrete. Coming in you have to stand naked in a circle of other women and police and bend over and spread your butt cheeks! Are you for real? The smell was horrendous! There were women who looked like men and women who were still on crack and crazy out of their minds.

The women who looked like men felt it was their job to pick who they were going to be with when the fresh meat came in. Most of the women going into the jail were dying to get picked! Every five minutes there was a fight and these women was fighting like men, with police jumping on them with Billy clubs to break it up. I saw the police throw pregnant women up against walls, one lost her baby. I saw one girl get her eye bitten almost literally out, the blood was ridiculous.

And the bus ride to court was the worst; the bus had the men in the back and the women up front. The women would get on the bus and show the men their tits, pussy and ass! These nasty heffas was pulling bloody tampons out to show them, the men would jack off and cum on the gate that separated them, it was unreal watching them act like this. When I got on the bus the men would scream at me to turn around, but I would sit as close to the bus driver as I could facing forward. They would yell "Hey bitch show me yo titties" or tell me to pull my dress up and show my pussy. All I could do was sit there and daydream about jumping off the bus and into someone's car as they drove me off to Mexico! It was all I could think about in all that chaos!

Ma was also taken there but Sybil Brand was a big place and she was in a different cell than me. The cell that I was in had 125 beds in it, bunk beds. All you could hear was women talking loudly, singing, screaming, arguing, and cussing each other out. It was depressing. When I first got there, I wouldn't eat anything or go to the bathroom, I just laid in the bed with the blanket over my head. Then the police made me get up to go eat, but I just pushed my food to the side and watched all the hungry women fight over my food.

Then one day, two weeks after being there I got up and "pow" I hit the ground. They took me up to the infirmary and I was dehydrated and impacted with poop because I didn't want to use the bathroom there. They made me take a laxative that made me so sick. I was pooping and vomiting all at the same time. Then after that, they realized that my blood was Rh-O- and next thing you know they were calling me to the infirmary twice a week taking my blood without my consent! I wasn't eating so it made me even more sick. I had to start eating the fruit to stop being dizzy all the time.

Ma and I had our case linked together and she had a record that was as long as the state of Texas. The FBI had been looking to catch her so they could finally give her time and put her away, of course, I didn't know all this. MM and Ma hired me an attorney and Ma was nervous because she didn't know if I was going to tell them everything, so she had her sister bringing me personal items and money to the jail.

My family would not come to visit me in jail. When my mom found out that I was in jail, she went and got Alysa and tried to make me sign over guardianship to her. She came to see me one time and brought Alysa to the jail. She had her nose so high in the air at me and told me how I was the devil and all this other crazy mess that I didn't want to hear. "All my life you have neglected me and now more than ever I need you to be a mother and help me!" But this time she really turned her back on me. She left me in that place and didn't offer me any type of help, didn't want to find out what was wrong with me, didn't offer to help me get an attorney or anything, she just wanted me to sign some papers so she could get a check for taking care of Alysa. I don't care if you feel your child is acting crazy or running wild and needs to learn a lesson, Sybil Brand was not the place to leave your youngest baby, anything could have happened to me in there. What kind of parent turns their back on their child in a situation like that? I was done with her.

The attorney that Ma and MM hired for me was a white guy and we thought he was on our side. He sent a Cease-and-Desist letter to the jail to stop them from taking my blood! Then he was bringing us cigarettes in jail that we would break down and sell. We made so much money doing that. I thought he was cool. I didn't know anything about court, lawyers, or judges, but when we went to court for the arraignment, I saw a whole different person! My attorney came to me and told me, "They don't want you, you're just a little fish in a big pond, it's her that they want", now you do want to go home, don't you? All you have to do is walk into the courtroom and say her name and you'll be home in time for dinner tonight" "I'll treat you to a lobster dinner, just do this for me".

I looked at my attorney in disbelief and he had this look in his eyes. Now I am the type of person that regardless of what, I will own up to my own actions, I'm not snitching. No one put a gun to my head and told me to do the things that I did, I did it of my own free will. I know most people would tell me that I'm crazy but I wasn't taking that route, not to mention that I ran with these people, and I saw some of the things they were capable of. I wasn't saying anything, my lips were sealed.

We're in court and the attorney tells the judge that I was prepared to give up my connection and all eyes were on me. My attorney looked at me and said "ok go ahead". I looked at him, shook my head, and said "I don't know what you're talking about" His whole face turned beet red and he looked like he was going to bust an artery "COME ON, JUST SAY IT, SAY IT" he was screaming at me in the courtroom. I just put my head down and the judge said "Miss Smith is this the decision that you're making" I looked up and said, "I don't know what any of you are talking about, but I gave my attorney my statement earlier and that's it". The judge said "Fine your choice!" My attorney stood up in the middle of the court and packed his briefcase, he said "I no longer represent Ellena Smith" and walked out of the courtroom! I was sitting in there with no attorney, he just left out, so the judge had to continue the case. And because the courts were pissed at me for not snitching, they continued the case, month after month after month!

I sat in Sybil Brand for what seemed like forever. I had to learn real quick how to survive in jail. I had gay women always hitting on me, but I had to buck up or they weren't going to leave me alone. This he/she came to the shower I was in and pulled the curtain open while I was in there naked! I had to react or else I was going to be somebody's bitch! I went off, I started talking real ghetto "bitch, don't you ever come at me like that, I ain't one of these punk ass gay bitches in here that you can try to run!" She started laughing at me and walked off, but guess what? She didn't mess with me anymore.

One of the police officers was one of my old high school friends and he was shocked to see me there. I was so embarrassed when I saw him, I told him some crazy story that a fraudulent credit card company gave me a bad credit card and I used it and got in trouble, of course, he didn't believe me, but he became my savior by setting me up in the computer lab helping the police type up documents and that got me out of the cell for most of the day. Then I asked him if he could transfer Ma to the same cell as me and he did. Me and Ma became very close.

Everyone in jail thought she was my mother. She was one of those old-school prisoners that everyone respected so she had food coming from the police cafeteria, and other inmates buying commissary for her, washing our clothes. Then she had an attorney friend who couldn't defend us because he had a drug problem, but he became our new cigarette connect. She would have me smuggle them in because no matter what happened in the cell, the police never messed with me. They had random searches where they would come in and tear up everybody's bed and personal belongings, looking for contraband, but my stuff never got touched. I had my Bible then had a Qur'an sent in and I would always leave them on my bed when I wasn't in the cell. I had a stack of cigarettes under my mattress and a Bible and a Qur'an on top of my pillow. One cigarette would break down into ten, and they sold for five dollars each, so you could imagine the type of money we were making off of them. We were the only inmates sending money out of the jail because you could only have a certain amount of money on your books.

Jail is crazy, women were making crack pipes out of tampon holders. They would swallow a balloon full of drugs and then poop it out! Ewwww! It was a full drug operation going on in this joint. I had to watch gay women having sex with each other, it was mostly oral and finger stuff, but you had no choice but to see it, each bunk was right next to each other. I just sat on my bunk, reading my Bible or my Qur'an, and thought about getting home to Alysa. I tried to stay away from all the foolishness that went on in there. I stuck out like a sore thumb in that place. I was clean, I had all my teeth, I wasn't sitting in circles loud talking, I didn't fight with anyone there. I made a few friends with the girls with big cases, and it's funny because I was in there so long that I watched people come and go. No one believed me when I told them I was in for forgery because most people committing forgeries were getting out within thirty days, three months at the max.

One day one of the officers walked by my bunk and looked at me and started talking to me. He asked why was I there and he told me I didn't look like I belonged in jail. He set me up to go to a computer class. An older black woman was teaching the class. She took me under her wing and she taught me MS-DOS, Word, and Excel. I ended up getting certified and received a certificate in computer applications. That move saved me from engaging in the cell because I started making friends with the murderers, they were the only ones that were in there as long as I was. And it also taught me a new skill!

I started to pray a lot because the only thing you could do in jail was read and try to get your life right with God. There was such a bad vibe in that place. I learned that so many women had killed themselves in there and at night when everyone in the cell was sleeping, I would hear low roar chatter. Some nights I could feel something breathing on me. I would just keep the blanket over my head, but I could feel something sitting on my chest, breathing in my face.

In Sybil Brand, my dark energy was able to mess with my mind the most. Because so many women had committed suicide in that place it was a scene that kept playing in my face like a movie. One night I got up to use the bathroom. The whole room was still. As I approached the bathroom area, I saw a white woman walking with a white gown on. I already knew what it was, but by now I was more curious to see how my sightings would play out, so I followed her. She looked at me and watched me as I followed with a little distance between us. She hit the corner and watched me as she turned, so I slowly followed behind her, when I hit the corner, she and three other women were hanging by sheets on the banister above the toilets, their bodies swinging.

This was the perfect environment for my dark energy to attack me. It constantly taunted me with dreams and full visions of me committing suicide. I now had visions of myself hanging in the bathroom, and I would wake up with a jolt crying and sweating. I only stayed sane by reading the Bible and the Qur'an. Like I said earlier, I've always had a strong spiritual connection with God and I have been open enough to see what other people can't see and I have seen some things. I read the Bible diligently and I participated in Ramadan! I put a light covering over my head and whenever my head was covered it eased my mind knowing that whatever I hear or see can't hurt me. I had to keep a lot of faith and trust in Him!

14. CRACK IS WHACK

I was arrested in August 1992, and now it was approaching August 1993. I missed my baby so much, a whole year without seeing her beautiful face. I was assigned a DA we finally went back to court and I was finally sentenced. The judge gave me eighteen months, the maximum sentence she could give on my charge, with prison time and twelve months served, so I had to go to Chowchilla. It is a maximum-security prison in Nor Cal. To be honest, I didn't care at this point; it was just a relief to get out of Sybil Brand. I only had a few more months of my sentence, but still in an effort to show me how pissed they were at me for not snitching they sent me to the A yard. A yard is where they send lifers, people who are not getting out of jail.

Everyone was shocked that they sent me there, even the police kept telling me "Do not tell anyone there how much time you have", they'll try to make you get more time or try to hurt you! That was the perfect thing for me to hear on my way up there. I was on the same yard as Susan Atkins, you know the Manson murders! NICE! My roomie was a double lifer, hard-core Chola, but she was cool, luckily God was with me. At least they had better food here. I lost so much weight at Sybil Brand; I was so skinny I looked like a crackhead! All the girls at Sybil kept saying I had AIDS, they claimed that you're supposed to gain weight in jail, but I wasn't eating that nasty food. I lived off the chicken that we got from the police kitchen and fruits and vegetables and I was working out.

When I got to Chowchilla, they gave me a job in processing so it made my time there go even faster. I was there for a few months, counting down every day to the release date they had given me. I was relaxed there because I had a release date, there was no fighting, and all the women were chill, they knew they weren't going anywhere so they just made that home and kept it clean and respected it. The police were not so hard-core here, so I just chilled until my date. I heard that the B and C yard was more turned up! Ma was sent to Chowchilla as well and she was on the B yard. We saw each other every day when we went outside or to meals. She kept telling me that she had enough money saved to open a beauty salon when she got out, that she didn't want to commit any more crime, and that I was set for life for not snitching. It sounded good, so I flowed with it.

My date finally came, I walked out of prison with nothing but the $300 they give you when you're released and the outfit that Ma's sister sent for me to wear out. My Aunt who lives in Modesto came and got me and shortly after we got to her house MM was right there. She cooked me the best meal I had ever had in life and after we ate, we left. Of course, we barely got to the freeway before we had to pull the car over! Hey, it had been over a year. I couldn't wait! He took me shopping and I stayed in Nor Cal for a few days but I was excited to get home to my baby girl.

When got back to San Dimas, I walked in the door and when Alysa saw me, she screamed and ran to me, jumped into my arms and we both hugged each other and cried. She said "Mommy don't ever leave me and go to school again" I looked confused! My Mom told her that I went off to college! Whatever I was just happy to be home! After MM dropped me off, I kept calling him and he wouldn't answer any of my calls, I was getting pissed. So, when he finally answered my call, I asked what was going on. He stayed down with me the whole time I was in jail, writing me letters, and coming to visit, so I thought he was fully invested. I told him that I wanted to be his wife and that I wanted to spend the rest of my life with him. He dropped a bombshell on me, he told me that while I was in jail he met someone and he was in love with her and they had a baby. I was crushed, this was some bullshit! Why didn't he tell me any of this before? That was the worst thing I could have been told!

Then my parents started tripping, telling me I had to do something with myself or get out. Damn, I just got out of prison a week ago, let me breathe! But I decided to go back to school for Cosmetology since Ma did say she was going to open a beauty salon; this would take my mind off MM and also give me the skills to do something within her shop. I went back to Citrus College and I hit it hard. I took Business as my minor with classes during the day and Cosmetology as my Major with classes in the evening. I was a straight-A student in every class. I made a friend in Cosmetology class and she was from Pasadena, so we started hanging out. I found out that she was also friends with MM's ex, the one he was with when I first met him. It was crazy because we all started partying together, but this time my partying was mild. Lisa was not as wild, she was classier and she acted older than her age. She was working as an assistant at a salon in Pasadena called Turning Heads and she got me a job there.

I used my financial aid money and got myself a car, I still had to use some of my skills to get the car though. I made a paycheck from scratch! I feel like I invented copy-paste lol. I got my car and everything was going so cool. Because I didn't snitch on Ma they couldn't give her much time, so a little after a year of my release, she was released. I had stayed in touch with her twin sister, the one who brought me clothes, and shoes, and put money on my books while I was in jail and I had grown real fond of her. She was so sweet! Ma's family took me in as their own and I would go hang out with them.

When Ma was released, I was only a semester away from my degree, yes, I turned a two-year program into 16 months and was close to taking the State Board Cosmetology test, but her release threw me off. She really did have a lot of money put away and her sister had been managing all her finances for her while she was in jail. She got out and got this beautiful condo right around the corner from my parent's house. My parents knew nothing about Ma because they never came to any of my court appearances; they just blamed everything on MM. So, when she moved into her condo, she set up a room just for me and Alysa. She bought me a bunch of clothes and shoes that I had to keep over there because I didn't want my parents questioning where I was getting all this stuff from. Well, I went from a straight-A student, getting offers to study abroad, to dropping out of school again, one semester away from graduating! But we started on the project.

We immediately went to LA and found a building to start up the salon. We went and bought a ton of building supplies, hired some day laborers, and the construction of Shear Joy Beauty Salon on the corner of Pico and Redondo was underway! I was on Ma's hip 24/7. We ate out at the best restaurants, again she was buying everything in the world for me and Alysa, but her son hated every bit of it! He was so jealous of me; that he tried to fight me. It was always a problem when he came around. I think MM was jealous of the relationship that Ma and I had also, but he was still friends with her and now I had to see him and his new bitch all the time and their baby. But do you think that a new girl in his life, that he was so in love with, stopped us from sneaking away every time we saw each other? Of course not! He and I had too strong of a connection, that's why I couldn't believe that he was doing this to me. All I could do was look my sexiest whenever he came around and it worked. But this little stupid girl had him tied around her little finger. He really liked her, and it was only because she was light-skinned with long hair, she wasn't that cute, but men confuse light skin with beauty. Anyway, I wouldn't date anyone I was just wrapped up in the salon and seeing MM here and there when I could.

The salon finally opened after a few bumps in the road, from someone stealing all the construction materials and Ma having to replace everything, to the plumbers installing the pipes wrong and having to bust the wall open to re-pipe it, to a shady electrician that did work so wrong it could have blown the whole building up! And then an almost robbery by gunpoint! God gave me strength that night to push and lock the door on 4 masked men with guns! This was our life, every day going to local shops, looking for the best stylist in LA, and buying salon equipment. Towards the end, as the deadline was approaching, the hired help wasn't moving fast enough so Ma got her family involved and we all got into the shop, painting walls, making stair banisters, and hanging high curtains on scaffolding. We put in every little detail in that shop, I put together the bathrooms, put in the cabinets, put up wallpaper, and I put every bit of blood sweat, and tears into that shop. We worked literally from sun up to past midnight every day.

That shop was the most beautiful thing I had ever seen. It had a crystal chandelier that hung high and glistened with the light of every passing car. Mirror everywhere and Marble floors. It looked like something that belonged in Beverly Hills. The shop changed her. It started to get a lot of attention, even before it opened. City Council Members invited her to dinners to say Thanks for fixing up the neighborhood, and her head swelled. Next thing you know, Ma was a Diva! She was a hardcore chick from the streets, quick to cuss a nigga out, but the salon was driving her crazy. This wasn't the streets. You can't come into the salon cussing out the stylist. Everybody was looking at her like she was crazy! And she knew it; she used to say "Nay Nay this shop is going to kill me!" It was too much for her. She was used to crime and dealing with men on the streets. She didn't know how to be a square and run a legitimate business. And the money wasn't coming in fast enough for her, so she took on another project, a deli, right next door to the salon. She was working herself to death.

I always looked for opportunities to get away from the shop because that place started to wear on me. Ma put so much responsibility on me with that damn place. I was 24 and knew nothing of running a business. I had to be there to open it and to close it. I had to handle all the paperwork. I had to deal with the vendors. I had to be there when she wasn't to manage the stylist, and I was doing hair and nails, yes unlicensed. So, every chance I got to leave, I was out.

One day I was just driving around LA and stopped at a gas station and this Lexus pulls up next to me. This yellow dude hangs out the window and says "What's up pretty girl, my boy wanna holla at you!" I looked and this guy got out of the car, Ray, I thought he was a Mexican, only brothers here. But he opened his mouth and I knew for sure he was a brotha! He told me that he worked with Charlie Wilson and that he wanted to take me out. He said they were doing a show in Santa Barbara and he wanted me to go with him. I said yes, I needed a getaway so we exchanged numbers, and he called me constantly from that time.

We went to Santa Barbara on the tour bus, and we sat in the back. On the drive up there, he kissed all over me and he asked me to give him head, I did and had no problem doing it. Then we stayed at a hotel on the water, went to the show, and it was all a wonderful weekend. When we got back, he called me and I took a day off work for him to come pick me up. This is where the fairy tale ended! The Lexus was rented, he lived with his Mama, and he picked me up in some old bucket Honda! I decided I was not going to judge him based on his finances, at that time money flowed. So, I was like whatever!

As Ray and I started dating MM and Ma told me they couldn't stand him, and Ma kept saying that she had seen him somewhere before. I got mad and thought she was tripping on some jealousy bullshit. But Ray didn't help any, he and Ma had a bad vibe between them, and then he picked up on me and MM. He started sending me gifts to the shop, just to show him that we were dating. He would send like five dozen roses, balloons, bears, and Ma said he was acting psychotic. Silly me I still thought she was tripping. Then one day MM called me and said "Did you know this fool is sitting around the corner from the shop spying on you". Still didn't think much of it, I liked the attention, then Ray called me, this was about two weeks into our dating and he told me that he had a surprise for me.

I couldn't wait to see it. He rolls up to the shop, he's standing there with his arms behind his back! I have my hands out like "Gimme Gimme!" This dude puts out his arm, pulls up the sleeve of his shirt, and in the largest old English letters he could get was my name misspelled, tattooed on his whole arm "ELAYNA" I really should have bailed out at this point, but I didn't. We moved in together! We got an apartment in Ontario. Ma told me that she didn't want Ray anywhere near her shop, and she told me if I was going to be with him, I couldn't come either! All the work I put in that damn shop and now I was just put out like a stranger. FINE! I was tired of that place anyway, but that was my income, what was I thinking to choose Ray over the Shop?

My Military sis and her husband had a baby together, but she soon discovered that her husband was an abusive jerk, as if we didn't see that coming! But she had to move so we all moved in together with Ray. Ray got a job driving limos and he was making pretty good money. Now the guy who was with Ray when I met him was Snook, his "brother". They are not really brothers but Snook was the only brother that Ray knew. He kept telling me

"I want you to watch out for Ray, he got that problem", and I really didn't know what he was talking about, I thought he was just trying to get me to not like Ray so I could sleep with him, that's always where my mind goes!

I found out the hard way what he was talking about. Ray would disappear on the weekends, he told me that he was in the studio with Charlie or at his friend D's studio, so I wasn't tripping too much until one day D called me and asked if Ray was home. "But I thought he was with you?" I said. He told me that he hadn't seen Ray in a while, so I was pissed. I went to do laundry, turned his pants upside down and an empty condom pack fell out of his pocket. Man, I was heated. This was a Friday, the whole weekend passed and I didn't hear anything from him. I started calling the hospitals, and the police department, I was really worried now. I thought something had happened to him! Sunday night the phone rings, and Ray is on the phone crying like a bitch! "I messed up, I should just kill myself" and I started crying with him, "No just come home and we'll work through whatever the problem is".

He gets home and announces to me that he has a crack addiction that he has been working on for the last seven years! "WHAT?" "CRACK?" shouldn't you have told me about this when we met? Then something clicked, Ma told me he looked familiar, well her son's father is a crack addict, so I called her and she told me "That's where I saw him, he was on the streets of Hollywood, doing crack with her son's father"! All I could do was shake my head, what have I gotten myself into? Things started coming up missing, like a ring that MB had given me, expensive clothes that Ma had bought me, and my CD collection that consisted of over one hundred CDs. I couldn't tell my sister; she would tell the family and I was too embarrassed for that. I didn't know that he was stealing money from her, she never told me.

Now for the whole time that I was with MM, we had sex constantly and I never got pregnant, so I went to the doctor and was told that it was unlikely for me to get pregnant again, I had too much scar tissue on my tubes to allow for sperm to pass. When I was pregnant with Alysa, I contracted genital warts and PID. I went to another doctor just for a second opinion and that doctor told me the same thing, so I thought I would never have another baby. But Ray was determined to get me pregnant, and it worked, I did get pregnant. MM and I would still have our occasional rendezvous, but Ma called me and told me that he had been arrested.

A little while before, MM was in San Dimas and got into a fight with some guy over money, and he was trying to scare the guy into paying him, so he shot a gun at the ground but the bullet hit the ground and shot up and hit the guy in the chest. The day that happened I went and got him and took him to LA and he was trying to lay low, I don't know what he was doing at the time he got arrested, but they got my baby and they weren't letting him out!

15. BREAKAWAY

On September 20th Symone Raevonn entered the world. She was Perfect! I was really happy to have her. After her birth, Ray's crack addiction took a serious turn for the worse. He stopped going to work so we lost our place. We moved to a cheap apartment in Fontana and my sis moved into the same complex different apartment. Every day that I had to wake up and see him lying in the bed next to me made me sick to my stomach. My sister got him a job working where she worked, but he was still disappearing on the weekends. At this point when he would call me and say he was going to kill himself, I would ask him if he wanted a gun or a knife. "Just do it already"! I still didn't tell anyone about him being on crack because my family really liked him. He was a different kind of crackhead. He was overly clean; he ironed his clothes just to go to the store. He was well-shaven and always kept up his appearance, so there was no way for anybody to know. Snook saw that finances were getting hard for us so he told him he could start going to Utah with him to buy Meth to bring back to Cali to sell. Well, that was a dumb move, not that Ray used Meth, but it gave him extra money to buy crack. We started fighting, real fights.

Ray tried to sell everything that was in our house, and when I would see him packing up electronics, I knew he was on his way to sell it for crack. He started packing up Alysa's Nintendo so I pulled a knife on him and we were fighting, with the knife in my hand. I wanted to stab him, but instead, I got cut and I was bleeding everywhere, so it stopped him that night. We fought so much, that my sister called the police on us, but that wasn't such a good idea, why me with scratches and him with a black eye! They wanted to arrest both of us. Poor Alysa, she had to be right in the middle of all this. We would fight and throw her toys at each other and she would sit there and scream "NOT MY BARBIE"!

Again, finances went into the dumps and we had to move yet again but this time we had no money so Snook and his wife offered to let us move into their home with them and we did. I hated Ray. I didn't want to sleep with him, I didn't want him to touch me. I had been locking him out of the room when we lived in Fontana, but now that we lived with Snook and his wife we had to sleep in the same room. Ray got mad that I wouldn't sleep with him and he was constantly trying to have sex with me, but I would burst into tears and tell him I was traumatized from being sexually abused as a little girl and raped as a young woman so he would back up and leave me alone. We didn't have sex for six months, and one day he came in the room, put his hand over my mouth, pinned me down, tore my clothes off me, and took it! I was so mad. We were pretty much over at this point, but I was not working, I had a little baby and Alysa so I couldn't just get up and leave.

We moved into an apartment in Corona and I started doing hair out of the house so I could save up some money. I also started skimming some money from his checks. Ray would get his check on Friday and I would have to take him to work, go with him to cash his check and he would tell me to hide the money so he wouldn't have access to it. A few hours later he would start tearing up the house, grabbing me by the arm and demanding me to give him his money. I couldn't fight with him anymore, I just gave it to him, and the money I was skimming I would put in the baby's diapers! If he ever changed her diaper I would have been in trouble!

I had to put a plan in place. Wait, where's my period? We haven't had sex, except that time he took it from me, it would be almost impossible for me to be pregnant from that 1 time! I went to the doctor and he told me "Congratulations you're pregnant!" I looked at him in shock and I said "How did this happen? He said "Well when you have sex" "No you don't understand, it was only one time!" and he said, "Well honey that's all it takes!" "Don't talk to me like I'm stupid, I know that"! I was numb! Now what am I going to do, another baby? I couldn't eat, I couldn't sleep, I was so sick and walking around in a daze. Ray started tripping, I think he knew that I was planning to leave him so he didn't want me to go anywhere. He took the car to work so I had no transportation. I had to walk Alysa to school and I had to walk to all my doctor's appointments. I hated my life at this point. I was about eight months pregnant and I was planning to go visit Tray but of course, Ray didn't want me to go, so he went to the car pulled all the wires out, and then started fighting with me while I tried to close the car door on him. He grabbed me by both my legs and pulled me out of the car and I fell to the ground right on my butt, 8 months pregnant!

Later that night I started having early contractions and went to the hospital. The baby didn't come that night so I had to tell my family what was going on because I had to get out of there. I told Ken and he came and helped me pack up my stuff while Ray was at work. I took everything except his clothes, and I cut up every picture of us together and left them scattered all over the place. We put my stuff in storage and I moved in with Tray, again. I don't know why but the night I went to the hospital to have the baby I called him just to let him know the baby was coming and he insisted on being there for the birth. I told him not to come to the hospital and that my sister was going into the labor room with me. He comes to the hospital high as shit, yelling and screaming at everybody, the nurses are telling me that I have to calm him down, so my sis said just let him go in the delivery room so he's not disturbing everyone. The day I left I dropped him off at work and took the car. I had bought new baby items for the new baby and I had a photo album filled with all of Symone's baby pictures in it, all in the trunk of the car. Ray said he was going to take the car and come back to get me when we got released from the hospital.

Imani Sherree was born on April 2nd. She was a beautiful baby, but out of nowhere, my newborn turned as blue as a Smurf, and was gasping for air! She lost almost all her oxygen! They did a code Blue on her! I had an elevated blood pressure so we had to stay in the hospital for a few days for observation. We were being released from the hospital a few days later, and no Ray! I tried to call him, no answer. The whole day almost passed and I just laid in the hospital bed crying and finally called my sister. She came and got us and took us back to Tray's house. He finally called me, crying, and told me that he lost the car, I couldn't believe it, with all my baby's pictures in it. He gave the car to some guy, who gave him some crack, in exchange for a car that had both our names on it! I never wanted to see him again.

He came to Tray's house, banging on the door, crying for me to let him in because he wanted to see his babies. I moved to my sister's house because I didn't want him to know where I was. Then one night my sis and Ken went to get some food and I was at the house with her husband, he was sitting there watching TV and I was on the couch feeding Imani and Ray just walked in grabbed Symone, and ran out the door. Imani was a little more than a week old and I couldn't move that fast. I put her down and ran outside down the stairs, I looked around and he was nowhere to be found. It was pouring rain outside and I sat there in the rain getting soaked. My sis still lived in the apartment complex that we had all lived in Fontana and we had friends there that Ray knew, so I went to their house to see if they saw what direction he went in, and there was that punk crouched down in a corner holding my baby. I snatched her from him and I didn't say a word to him. It was clear I had to move again, so I went to the house that he was afraid to go to, my Momma!

The first thing my mom said was "I dare him to come over here" and I guess he already knew because he never once came to her house or called over there. Ray was completely out of my life! By this time Alysa was in fifth grade and had already been to 7 elementary schools and now she had to go to another. My Mom was so mean to us while we were there, well not Alysa, that was her favorite grandchild. Symone was a crier and Mom couldn't stand my baby, she said "I can't stand Symone" so that was a big problem. We fought all the time. She made it as miserable as possible for me to be there. I just laid on the sofa, with Symone and Imani laid out on me and I wouldn't get up to do anything. I think I was still in shock about Imani. I didn't process all of this too well.

Ken had moved to Las Vegas and he got a job as a limo driver, but he had some issues with his driver's license that he had to come back to California to work out. He came and stayed at Mom's house and he saw me, just lying on the couch with my, as he called them "cubs" laid out on me. I gained so much weight with back-to-back babies, I had swelled to a whopping 210 pounds, coming from a steady 135 all my life. He told me "You really should move to Vegas with me". He said what are you doing with yourself? You look depressed and Mom is on your ass constantly. What's your reason for staying here? I thought about it, and the next day Symone was in the backyard playing and she kept touching my mom's roses, and Mom sneered at her "Leave my roses' alone", Symone was two, so she touched them again and she cut her finger pretty deep on a thorn, and my mom smirked at her and said "hum, that's what you get!" As my baby's finger bleed and she was screaming. I went off "What kind of Grandmother are you, you are so mean" and she told me "If you don't like it get out of my house!" At that moment I was ready to leave and I swore I would never speak to her again! She was dead to me! So, me and the kids were Vegas-bound. I was excited and scared to move to Vegas, of course, we had visited many times, and my Military sis had been stationed there and she liked Vegas, but I was moving out here not knowing anyone, no family, just me, Ken, and the kids.

16. VEGAS BABY

Ken was staying in a weekly hotel on Fremont St, in the middle of Downtown when we arrived in Vegas, in the ghetto! But he quickly started making a lot of money with the limo thing. Every night he came in with a pocket full of tips. I had to get on public assistance so I could have some income, and with our combined income, we had enough to move into a nice apartment on a better side of town. Things were going so good, I was finally happy! We had so much fun living together, going to Circus Circus, and all the other amusement-themed hotels on the strip. Ken treated me and the kids so well. He took us out to eat all the time and he encouraged me to eat healthy and start losing weight. We became vegetarians and experimented with many fruits, vegetables, and pastas. We started eating fine cuisine and playing with new dishes. I watched a lot of cooking shows and expanded my cooking talents. I always loved to cook but I was just lazy and didn't want to do it, but now I looked forward to preparing dinner for the family to see their reaction on whether they liked it or not, and every night started to become a hit! I was going to the Mosque with Ken and same as before, I liked the message that was being delivered, but the people, especially the women were not so friendly.

Now here was my issue with the church. As a young girl, I never could understand how people could come to church dressed in club clothes, drunk, or leave church and get drunk. And as a 9-year-old I read in the Bible, and in Leviticus, it tells you not to touch swine, but every Sunday, when church was over, we would always go to the social room for a rib dinner or pig feet. Then when we went to church in Victorville, I was violated. There was a couple there, and every Sunday the wife would get the "Holy Ghost" and do flips down the aisle, while her husband, the Usher sat in the back slumped over drunk.

One day I was in the nursery watching the babies, I was 13, I bent over to pick up a baby out of a playpen, and I felt someone standing right up against my butt, there was the Usher, he had an erection, and rubbed up against me and felt me up and down. I was shocked, and he just walked away. I could smell the old alcohol on his breath. Then My mom had us go on a snow trip with the church to Big Bear and while I was there one of the ministers flirted with me the whole time, tried to kiss me, and wrote his number in my Bible for me to call him. Again, I was 13! I was pretty much done with the church after that and I didn't want to go back.

For a while Mom forced us and little by little Ken and I stopped going with her. Learning about Islam was very welcoming to me, and the fact that the Nation of Islam was teaching self-awareness to black people and teaching us to love our blackness, is something I didn't grow up with. I was teased for being black and having nappy hair and thick lips, so to finally hear that my features were features of beauty and to know that women of other races spend money to get what I have naturally was a self-image boost that I needed. But I had a problem hearing how the white man is holding black people back because I grew up in a house where my parents worked and they never let anyone hold them back from anything, whether it be education or work.

My stepdad used to tell me "If you want to fly to the Moon, go join the military, get an education, join NASA, and take yo ass to the moon!" So, I did have a small problem with that part. I didn't go to the Mosque regularly, because like I said I didn't feel welcome. Although the church has its issues, the people make you feel welcome, because everyone in the church is equally messed up and they have no room to judge. The people in the Mosque always acted as if they were better or on a higher level because now, they had dropped their ghetto mentality and picked up a few books and read something that made them feel more educated, but I found out, for some it was all an act!

I had a problem when I first moved to Vegas. I didn't realize it was so racist! I was out here fighting in these Vegas streets. I'm lucky I didn't go to jail, but white women were so bold in Vegas. And I just came off the streets of LA so I wasn't having it. One day Ken came home from work and he said "I think I met my wife today!" He told me that he had met a beautiful girl working at the Luxor, with a British accent and long beautiful hair, and she was a Muslim. He started dating her right away. He really wanted me to meet her so he set up for all of us to meet at Circus Circus. She was so sweet and very proper, and her children a boy and a girl addressed her as "Mother". I was like "WOW" she really is a good girl and she might be good for my brother.

Sady, Ken's new girlfriend, invited us all to her house for dinner, she had a nice two-story home in Sunrise Mountain, she answered the door in an outfit that came up to her neck and long pants on and she said "Greetings" when she opened the door. She was an MGT at the Mosque, her home was spotless, with white furniture and plants all over while a waterfall trickled in the corner. There was beautiful classical music playing and hors d'oeuvres tastefully set on the table. It was such a beautiful serene display. Her children sat on the floor playing a board game peacefully together. Then I looked around, and thought to myself, this isn't real, it can't be. Nothing is this perfect, something weird is going on here. I offered to take out the trash, and when I went to the back, in the trash were empty boxes of the appetizers that she had just explained to me how she had made by hand, hmmm! And I started to notice that her British accent was fading as the night went on, oh and when I asked her what part of London she was from, she couldn't even give a fake answer! And sorry to tell you this bro, but her long hair is a weave. Come on I do weaves; I know a weave when I see one! Ken will tell you I circled her like a vulture and in a playful move I yanked her braid, hahaha! I can't remember all the details!

Her sister Tina was at dinner, she lived with Sady and she was really nice as well. After I exposed Sady, she lightened up a tad, she and Tina became my best friends. I would take my kids over to play, and just like typical Muslim women they acted as if they were better than me. Yeah, I cussed, I'm from the streets, and my stepdaddy spoke worse than a pimp on the streets, but they would hear me curse and put their hands over their mouths and say "Oh my", or if I said the word "kids" they would say we don't call our children kids, that's what you call baby goats. Oh My GOD!!! Get over it. One day as we sat eating dinner, Sady's daughter put her hands in the air and said "It's Mr. Nasty time!" Me and Ken looked quickly at her with puzzled looks on our faces and Sady smacked her in the mouth so fast. Now if I'm not mistaken, that's a line from the movie Next Friday, starring Ice Cube and last time I checked that wasn't a wholesome family movie.

Little by little Sady's perfect cover started to unravel, but Ken couldn't see it because this was his first time being in love and he thought she was PERFECT! Ken and I had shared an apartment and living expenses and we shared his car. I went out and found a job working at a Wedding Chapel, I had just started and could not afford the apartment that we had together by myself, but one day out of the blue in the middle of the month my brother came to me and tells me that he's moving in with her.

Two things here, first of all, he told me that he was hardly home and he's not running up the bills like me and the kids do, and that he wasn't going to be able to help me with the upcoming rent, next thing, Ken and Sady considered themselves Muslims and Muslims don't generally just move in together, there is a process in the Mosque considered a courtship where you have to date first, then once married you move in together. I was a little confused because Sady was supposed to be a respectable figure in the Mosque and she spoke as if she was so pure and holy. Now she was pulling this ghetto move, letting a man move into your home. Whatever that's pretty much the story of most Muslim women that I have met, they pretend to be so perfect and snub their nose at you, then turn around and shock your socks off, but I guarantee you this is only the beginning.

Sady and Tina were from San Bernardino CA and they moved to Vegas about the same time that I did. They still had family in San Bernardino. It started with Sady telling Ken that her mom was going to move in because she had a drug problem and they needed to get her away from San Bernardino, then she asked me to drive to Cali with her because her grandmother was smoking crack too. Her eighty-year-old Grandma's thirty-year-old Mexican boyfriend was tripping, when we got there, she was scouring the ground for a piece of crack she had dropped, so they wanted Grandma to move to Vegas as well. But when we got there, Grandma refused and said she wasn't moving to Vegas.

Her Grandma was so feisty but she was the sweetest thing you would ever meet in life. You could tell she was a roughneck, but she was quick to greet you and make you feel like you were family and ready at a moment's notice to pull out a pan and fry up some fish for you. She lived in a rough part of town and her home looked like it was still in slavery times, there was no toilet, just a hole you had to pee in where it looked as if a toilet did at one time exist in that spot. Chickens running all over the place and the living room was a makeshift bedroom.

This did not fit the image that Sady and Tina had portrayed of themselves, remember she told Ken she was British! Next to move in with Sady and Ken was her uncle. Freshly out from prison, but still addicted to drugs. He was a very big man with an insanely deep voice, he was a little scary-looking. Then came her brother who was also on that stuff, but he had poor health and he was very sick, he also brought along his girlfriend and their one-year-old baby. So, in their house was Ken, Sady, her two kids, sister Tina and her son, their Momma, Uncle, brother, his girlfriend and their one-year-old baby. Not quite what Ken had expected! You see we were soon to discover that Sady was a pathological liar. Even after moving, Ken was still sharing his car with me so that I could drop the babies off at daycare and get to work, but one day Sady asked Ken if she could use the car and he said yes. I called Ken and told him I had to go to work, but she cried to Ken that I had cussed her out and told her that I controlled Ken and he did whatever I told him to do. Of course, he called me and he was mad at me and told me to take the car to her. I was so hurt.

I couldn't believe that he would believe this lie that she was telling. I was like "Ken, you know me better than that, you know I would never say anything like that!" Then Ken busted out yelling at me that I always try to control him and that I even tried to control him when we were kids, and then he told me "You even spoke up for me when I was a kid and I didn't even want you to!" Man was I pissed! Do you know if I hadn't spoken up for you when we were kids Mom would have never done anything for you and now, you're using this against me like I did something bad to you! We got off the phone and I didn't talk to my brother again. Now I had to take a bus to drop the girls off at daycare, then I had to take a long walk to the next bus stop to catch that bus to work. Alysa had to walk herself to and from school, and I was never around to make sure she was getting there or back home OK, I just had to trust her. I was in a strange city, alone, just me and my babies!

17. THE KILLER IN ME

One day I was home and I got a call from my oldest sister. She informed me that my older brother was on a bus passing through Vegas and she asked me if I could pick him up, well I assumed that he was going to come to the house for a minute and then be on the next bus to California, so I said OK. They didn't tell me that he was coming in from Georgia and no one wanted him to stay at their house. He asked me if he could stay for a few days because he had to go to the doctor to get some stitches removed. Apparently, he was with some girl in Georgia who tried to kill him and stabbed him several times, then he started having seizures due to his heavy drinking. He told us that he had blacked out and fell on the concrete and hit his head, thus the stitches, but it looked more like knuckle marks more so than concrete.

His stay turned from days into weeks but during the time he was there he helped me through a few crazy situations like the day Alysa came in the house from playing, frantically crying, and told me some Mexican man had touched her in her privates, and of course, my reaction was going outside with a baseball bat firmly attached to my hands, and when she showed me his car I jumped on the top of the car and fully lifted the bat, I was just about ready to swing the bat into the windshield when my brother pulled up and yelled: "STOP!" He talked me down and convinced me to call the police. And the time when the police came to my door and asked me if I was the parent of Alysa Smith, I said "Yes" and he said, "Don't panic, but your child was just hit by a truck!" I PANICKED! I ran through the house screaming like a crazy woman and luckily, he was there, he went to the scene because I had the babies. She was hurt but not bad, but the situation was handled calmly.

Anyway, on the flip side, his ass was a dirty filthy alcoholic. He woke up and ate cereal with alcohol, he laid on the sofa all day stanking with a bottle of whiskey in his hand, and then he sat up all night and drank. At first, he kept asking me "Let me hold something" to buy his alcohol and cigarettes, but that got real old. Then he starts working at a day laborer place making 30 dollars a day, just enough for his habit, but not enough to leave. This was not what I wanted my girls to see, not to mention I was very uncomfortable leaving my children in the house with him. Then I had to change my work hours so Alysa could watch her sisters, it was way too hard trying to do this on the bus. Eventually, I bought a little bucket for $400.

So, I come home from work one day, he is passed out on the sofa, Alysa is doing the dishes and won't turn around and Symone is standing by the door of the girl's bedroom crying. Tell me why do I hear my baby Imani inside the room screaming her head off? I open the door; my baby's diaper is off and she is standing in a pile of poop! She is shaking and her face is as red as a beet, obviously from crying for so long. I went to Alysa first, and she told me he told her she better not open the door for Imani, as a matter of fact, don't even turn around and look at the door. All I could see was RED! I walked over to him, he was passed out on the sofa with the remote clutched in his hand. I grabbed the remote to the TV out of his hand, but before I knew it, he had snatched it back from me so fast I hardly knew that I had grabbed it. I told him "Give me my remote and get your shit and get out of my house", he just looked at me and said "Nope!" And rolled over and went back to sleep.

So, I tried to grab the remote again and he pushed me. I grabbed the remote and threw it at him. (But in my head, I went to the kitchen and I grabbed a knife. I pretended to fall towards him and the knife went into his chest, he stumbled and fell on the floor. I started stabbing him over and over, and I was covered in his blood. I held up the knife which blood was dripping from, and I looked down at his lifeless body. But then I looked at my children! They looked in horror as they screamed in fright). I really wanted to kill him, but I snapped back and realized I was getting way too mad, so I thought sensibly, and I called the police. When they came, they told me because he had established residence at my home, they couldn't put him out and that I would have to evict him.

This was preposterous! But they said because he was so drunk they had to take him to 24-hour lock-up detox, and it was my option to do whatever I wanted to do at that point, wink wink. They handcuffed him and he tried to tell them to arrest me for assaulting him by throwing the remote at him, they just laughed and took his butt to jail. I immediately rolled up all his shit and put it in trash bags and sat everything outside the door. He got out about five o'clock in the morning and he was banging on my door to let him in, I just ignored him, put my earplugs into my ears, and dozed off peacefully to sleep. The damn phone rings and it's my mom, she had the audacity to tell me "If you don't get up and let your brother in the house", I told her "Better yet why don't I buy him a Greyhound ticket to your house and you can pick him up and let him in at your house?" You know what she said to me "SHIIIIIITTTTT, he ain't coming here!" I said "Oh really, well goodnight then" I hung up the phone and after a while the knocking stopped and I didn't see him again!

I was still working at the Chapel, it was such an exciting job, all kinds of people from all kinds of places came through there to get married. Celebrities, naked people from the porn conventions, people in costumes. It was crazy, and the owner was a character herself. She had a crazy crackhead son that constantly stole money from her whenever he got the chance to, so there was a strict "No Chipper (the nickname of her son) on the premises rule" enforced! She had three chapels, the famous one on Las Vegas Blvd, a little tacky one Downtown, and a big one at a Casino Hotel. I pretty much became a supervisor of the Downtown chapel and that's where I worked most of the days. I made pretty good money with the chapel, but for some reason, I discovered that she didn't have a good system for her inventory, and on days when I needed some extra spending cash, I would sell a video or something small and just pocket the money. She never knew and it was just a few dollars here and there, all and all, still, it was wrong, but I thought what the hell.

One day I got a call from one of my friends at the main chapel and she said "You would never guess who's in here getting married. Your brother!" I couldn't believe it Ken was marrying Sady and he didn't even tell me about it. I thought whatever I didn't want to go to their stupid wedding anyway! I was hurt. Then a few weeks later Sady's sister Tina came into the Downtown chapel and she was getting married, to some guy she had met at the Mosque. I no longer had Tina to hang out with, besides when me and Ken got into our fight, I had stopped talking to all of them anyway, so I just started hanging out with people from work, drinking again, going to strip clubs and I even got my first tattoo! I was running wild, as usual, but I didn't know what else to do.

At work, I never saw any men, occasionally you get a good-looking best man you can flirt with, but one day I came to work and there stood this tall, bald, fine, caramel complexion man in a suit, I had to do a double take. He walked over to where I was, opened the door for me, and said "Hello" in a fine Barry White tone, "I'm RB, I'm a new limo driver here, what's your name?" I had to close my mouth and come out of shock because he really was that fine. He looked like a model on the cover of GQ magazine. The next few days we spent a lot of time together because ironically, I was training him. I had learned every aspect of the Wedding Chapel and I moved from the Downtown Chapel and was given a lot of responsibility with the main chapel. RB started making good tips as a driver and soon he was taking me out to lunch or dinner almost every day. We weren't officially dating we just hung out a lot. Alysa came home from school one day and said "Mommy Sady's pregnant, and she's big like the baby is due soon!" A friend of hers knew Sady's little sister (her mother's stepdaughter from her new marriage) and they told Alysa. Man, my brother is going to have his first baby? There was no way in the world I was going to miss that.

So, after almost a year of not talking to my brother, I went to their house one day with a stack of old mail and rang the doorbell. Sady answered the door with a belly looking like it was ready to pop! I used the mail as an excuse to come over, and when Ken came down the stairs and saw me, his face lit up probably as bright as mine did. We hugged for a long time and he couldn't wait to sit down and talk to me and tell me everything that had been going on in his life! I joined back in with the family as if I had never left. By this time Ken and Sady had rolled up every member of her family and got them out of the house. They all found apartments in Vegas. Ken had something he wanted to ask me but he was so reluctant to bring it forward. Then he took me to his room and showed me a letter and he asked me "Did you type this letter and forge this signature?" It was a letter from the main Mosque in Chicago granting Ken his X. A little history, when Ken got into the fight with the police back in the day, the Mosque wouldn't grant him his X, it was political, so one day Sady gave Ken this letter telling him that he had gotten his X (to change his name from Smith) because that was the only way that they could get married. He took the letter to the Mosque and they looked at Ken like he was crazy because they knew it was falsified.

When Ken asked Sady about the letter, she told him that she came to me and told me about their problem and I made the letter! EXCUSE ME! First of all, I haven't talked to you guys for almost a year and secondly, I'm a master forger and I would never do something so sloppy! Then it all came out, he started telling me everything about Sady, how she is always lying about everything, that she is really ghetto, and how everything he thought about her was fake. I was like Man I could've told you that! Then he apologized for the car incident because as he discovered that his wife was a compulsive liar, he realized that she had made that whole story up and was feeding him lines about me being controlling to him. Her family kept telling Ken that she was tricking him with that innocent shit. Her whole family was ghetto, how could she try to pretend that she was proper? He was in too deep now to go anywhere, they had a baby on the way and Ken was very excited about that.

18. NOT WHAT IT SEEMS TO BE

My niece Du'hara Muhammad was born on March 28th. She was absolutely a beautiful baby, and as I do with all the babies, I instantly fell in love with her. Sady had a terrible C section and she could hardly get around, so I would come over in the mornings after working all night to help with the baby, but she would stay in her room all day until Ken came home from work to relieve me so that I could go get ready for work. After Sady got back on her feet, we started hanging out a lot and her family became my family. She always wanted to go shopping and go eat! Somewhere along the way, I felt that shopping was more important than paying my bills and I was shopping with her all the time until finally I got evicted from my apartment. I was still seeing RB and I moved in with Ken and Sady. But I lost my mind, I spent so much time with RB, after work, I would go spend the night at his house while I abandoned my kids at Ken's house.

Sady was getting sick of that and she was ready for us to move out, but I didn't have a place yet and my credit was shot so it wasn't easy for me to get into a place, so me and the kids moved into a weekly hotel. I tried not to leave the kids at the hotel by themselves too much but RB and I had such a great sex life it was hard to resist him. Although it was a very strange sex life, he liked to play rape where he would tie me to the bed and blindfold me, leave me there for about an hour, sneak in the room, and violently tear my clothes off and have violent sex with me. He was tearing up some of my good stuff!!! But it was fun. He also liked to pretend that I was a prostitute, he would have me dress in a hoe outfit, wait on the corner for him to pick me up, take me home, and treat me like a hoe. I was very attracted to strange sex because of my trauma, I liked the whole play rape thing, go figure??

Well Sady had a brother named GQ who was living in an apartment that he was moving out of but the lease wasn't up so he offered to sublease it to me! It was perfect, I didn't have to qualify and we could just move right in. When I moved in, RB's lease was up on his apartment and he needed a place to stay, so he asked if he could move in as a roommate, although we were sharing a room and a bed. I thought to myself this will be perfect, I'll make him fall in love with me and then I can have the relationship with him that I've wanted to have. I kept asking him why he didn't want to have a relationship with me and the only answer he gave me was "It's complicated" and boy was I about to find out just how complicated it was.

Now GQ is a pretty boy, fine face, and sculptured body, Mr. Playboy! Anyway, because of the situation, me living in GQ's apartment RB always thought something was going on between us. One day as I sat in the house watching TV there was a knock at the door, this woman with locs stood at the door and asked me "Are you Ellena?" Already I knew this was someone that RB was messing with, she knew where I lived and she knew my name. She said, "My name is Keke and I wanted to come tell you that me and RB have been messing around and when you're at work he has me over here!" That Muthafucka!!! I was so mad, so I invited her in and I said "Well come on in, he should be home from work any minute and I know he would just love to see you here!" We talked and she told me she didn't know about me at first and that she met RB while they worked together at the convention center.

The key hit the door and the door knob turned, in walked RB not yet looking up, I said "Hi sweetieeeeeeeee!!!!" He looked up and his mouth hit the floor when he saw me and Keke sitting there together. Of course, he went off on her for being there and made her leave so he could explain to me how crazy she was. Telling me of her crazy relationship with her abusive boyfriend. Whatever, she knew where I lived. Now this is where it gets funny. Keke kept calling me and tried to chum up to me. She came over one day and she said I know this apartment all too well, didn't a guy named GQ live here? A surprised look came over my face and I said "Why yes, what did you sleep with him too?" And much to my surprise she said "Yes!" All I could think was "You little hoe". So now RB thought me and Keke had both slept with GQ, even though I kept telling him that GQ was like family, he still said it made him uncomfortable.

Ken had started a moving business and he would go move furniture for people. Well, one of his moves was moving Keke out of her apartment with her abusive boyfriend. Vegas is too small! Her man kept telling Ken and Sady's brother "Yeah if you talk to her long enough, she'll give you some pussy! She gone try to pay for this move with a threesome!" So, Sady's brother got Keke's number, and passed it to GQ who took her out and they ended up sleeping together. I was in some sort of weird triangle. Keke had moved out from her boyfriend and she was living in a hotel but she was getting kicked out of the hotel so my stupid ass let RB convince me to let her stay with us for a couple of days until she found a place. How was I so stupid? But like I said before, we weren't in a relationship, he reminded me we were "roommates" and he told me that if she didn't move in, he was going to go with her to a weekly. If I was smart, I would have let him go with her, but he was helping with the bills. I was so crushed, what did he see in this little tramp??? But I agreed and just like I thought when I was gone to work, he was fucking this bitch in my bed, duh!

At that time, I really thought I was in love with RB and I basically let him control me. Oh, did I mention that he was a big weedhead? He smoked weed day and night, anyway I come home from work one night, he had put the kids to bed and he and Keke were high off their asses! Everything was dark except the light from the TV, when I saw the scene, I had a major attitude. Before the words "I want her out" could roll off my lips RB grabbed me and started kissing me. Before I knew it, he had my clothes off and threw me down on the bed. He asked me "Can Keke eat you while you give me head?" I was trying to say "hell no" but she had already started. Then RB was in me while eating on her! It was a crazy freak scene. I started drinking and we had this wild crazy threesome all night.

RB thought this was going to be the idea set up, but the next day when I woke up, I said I wanted her out. Keke wasn't expecting that so started flipping out and she jumped on RB and started hitting him. He grabbed her by the arms, she fell to the ground and got loose. I went after her and she swung her purse at me but instead of hitting me, Imani was coming down the hall and she hit my little Imani in the head with her purse! I lost it! I saw a wine bottle, I grabbed it, busted it in half on the wall, grabbed Keke by her neck, dragged her body up the wall, drew back with the broken bottle and when I swung it around before it could slice her neck RB had snatched the bottle out of my hand. He yelled, "She isn't worth it!"

He grabbed Keke, threw her out the door, closed it, and locked it. Then we gathered all her clothes and threw them out from the patio! Gees Louise!!!! I had a bad tendency of almost blacking out when I got mad and something would completely take control of me and make me want to kill. I thank God for always being that force in my life putting people in my path that prevented anything like that from happening. As crazy as it sounds, I understand why some people commit murder. If you have demons, it's not you in your right mind! I needed help but didn't recognize it!

RB and I continued to live together, and he told me why we couldn't be in a relationship with me. He was married and his wife cheated on him with a woman! She divorced him and moved to Vegas. He was only here hoping to convince her to leave her girlfriend and get back with him. He was still in love with her and he wasn't giving up trying to get his wife back! How was all this going on and I didn't see any of it? One day he asked if his cousin could come visit for a while. My fire for him was starting to dwindle because I saw this situation was a dead-end road.

His cousin arrived and he was a very handsome guy, although he was a little shorty. We all took a trip to California and I had left the kids with Ken, we just rode out to go to the beach and sightsee. His cousin kept flirting with me and I was flirting back with him. When we got back home RB said my cousin wants to fuck you, I want you to give him some while I watch. I was like "Are you sure that's what you want?" And he said yep! His cousin's size was so massive, like something totally unreal. He was too big and it hurt so bad. When we were done, I was really in pain.

The next day I was rolled into a ball bent over on the bed with a fever and I was shaking. For the last few months, I had a period but it was a weird one each month, similar to when I was pregnant with Alysa. Like, it only lasted for two to three days whereas my periods usually lasted seven to eight days. RB and his cousin were going back to California and I told him I was really sick and not to leave me and he left anyway. I didn't want to go to the doctor because what was I gone tell them "I had a big dick in me and it made me fall ill!". So, I stayed home in excruciating pain then suddenly I felt a gush from my vagina and I got up to run to the bathroom and there was blood everywhere, running down my leg. I made it to the toilet and I felt a small contraction. I looked in the toilet and lo and behold it was a fetus! It was maybe about 12 weeks. I was sitting on the toilet and I started throwing up all over the floor. I wanted to pick it up to look at it but I couldn't.

What the hell is my life? I couldn't even believe that I had been pregnant through all of this! Of course, I had to call in sick from work, and I just laid in bed for the rest of the day. RB called me that night to ask me how I felt and I told him "I had a miscarriage." He really didn't have much of a reaction to what I had just told him and he said OK I'll see you tomorrow. When he got home, he had no compassion for me and what had happened instead he looked at me and said "I can't believe you fucked my cousin!" (Same scenario as with MM) I just looked at him and I asked him "Are you on crack?" He said to me, "Now I know I could never have a relationship with you after this" I didn't care at this point, I was just like "WHATEVER". I had already talked to GQ and he told me the lease was nearing an end, so I went out and found a house, and I told RB "I'm moving into a house and you're not coming with me." He said oh I was planning on leaving anyway, so cool.

The day came that he was packing his stuff to leave and he had the nerve to ask me if he could have some goodbye sex, I just looked at him and rolled my eyes, and next thing you know he was charging after me. I ran to the room and locked the door, but very effortlessly he busted the door off the hinges, he jumped on my back, pinned me down and started tearing my clothes off. Now ordinarily this is about the way that we had sex, but I was not feeling him at this moment. So, I told him to get off me, but he grabbed me by my hair and smashed my face into the pillow, and fucked me from behind. It reminded me so much of the time I was raped by the guy in Ladera Heights and I panicked. I couldn't breathe and suddenly I was having an asthma attack. He looked at me and he felt so bad, he found my inhaler.

After I got my breath through all my tears, he grabbed me and held me and he held me for a long time. At that moment I wished he would have smacked me in the face and just walked out the door, because when he held me, it felt so good but I knew there was nothing more that we could do with each other. He kissed me grabbed his bags and left. I just sat on the bed and cried. I was so mad because if he had just left without all the drama then it would have been easy for me, but seeing his show of emotions let me know that he did care about me. Is there something wrong with me? Am I not marriage material? Does every guy that I'm with just see me as something sexual? I didn't get it, but hey life goes on.

19. PIMPING AIN'T EASY

Me and the kids moved into our new home and after 2 years of employment, I felt it was time for me to move on from The Wedding Chapel. I had gotten so deep into stealing money from them, that it felt like an addiction. I stole money even when I didn't need to and I couldn't stop. Then Valentine's Day came, the busiest day for the Las Vegas Wedding industry. That day I sold so many wedding packages and extras, and I also put about $900 cash in my pocket. I was so nervous that I had made plans to quit after that. The next day the owner called me into her office and she told me that I had marked a video sold but the money collected was short. Here's the irony, on that particular wedding I did collect the money so I had the nerve to get an attitude, and I told her "If you're gonna treat me like a thief and not trust me then I don't need to be working for your company!"

She asked me not to quit, but I walked out of there in a huff, then she came after me and said "I want you off my property right now!" See she was the type that wanted to look as if she always had the upper hand, so she made it look like she fired me rather than me quitting on her. I didn't care I already had another job lined up. In the next few days, I went to CLS, Limo Service and I started working as a limo driver, just like my big bro! My boss was an older Caucasian, white-haired man. It was hilarious at first hearing him talk of how he likes his coffee dark and the darker the berry the sweeter the juice. And I just laughed at him at first, but then he started to get a little out of line with the comments telling me how he likes big booties and then he started touching my butt and tracking my every move.

This job was nothing but men, so being flirted with was a daily occurrence for me. The white guys, the Ethiopians, the Mexican guys, and of course all the brothas, I was the sexiest limo driver there was. I was making money hand over fist. My tips were so ridiculous, I drove everybody, singers, rappers, TV show hosts, and athletes, but my biggest tips came from the no-name regular Joe. I had guys requesting me as their driver and would tip me very generously. I started off doing my job as I was supposed to, then I met Ant. He was from Pasadena and he knew DJ, Alysa's father, and all the Party Boys so we instantly became friends. Ant was so fine; he had a short stint with the Dodgers but it didn't work out for him and some kind of way he ended up in Vegas. He used to tell me "Girl you my folks, you know I'm gone look out for you. How much money you taking home each night?" I replied "I don't know, maybe $200 or $300" he said, "Please that's chump change, I'm finna show you how to make some real money". Who could argue with that? First, he showed me what everybody was doing, stealing rides. We grabbed people from all over the strip when we were supposed to be on break or staging (waiting for the next ride), and then it got worse.

This was Vegas, and every time someone got into my limo they would say "Limo driver, where the girls at?" So, Ant told me every time someone asked me that, to call him. At first, he set everything up, he didn't want me to get too involved, but you know me, I'm a big girl, I can handle this, I got too involved! Next thing you know I had three girls that dealt with me exclusively, pahaha I was a pimpette! I would call them and tell them how far out I was, and they better be ready. I collected all the fees and paid them when I dropped them back off! Real pimp shit! Then the guys started asking me where can they get "Blow", so I called Ant. He told me to bring them to a place that became known as "The Spot." He would meet me there so I didn't have to handle anything, but I started to feel bold enough to do it on my own. OH MY GOSH! I'm being a pimp and now a drug dealer. I picked up balls of cocaine wrapped in plastic wrap, in a paper bag! I tried not to look at it too much! You know I hate drugs and I never wanted anything to do with them, but this was big money, and I'm fueled more by money than emotions! You know, I didn't think of myself as being a pimp and a drug dealer at first, but I evaluated the risk that I was taking and I got scared, but me being me, had gotten so addicted to the money I couldn't stop.

One night I had a wild group of white boys get into my limo and the usual questions of "Where do we go to get high and get laid" came up, "Boys, I got you!" I set everything up myself and made all the money, except one of the guys liked me and he sat up front with me. He offered me to hit his line, "Wigga please!" When the other guys went up to the room with the girls he wanted to stay in the limo with me. He was irritating the crap out of me, but I couldn't be rude, that's how I made my money, by making the guys like me. He's sitting in the limo with me and I said "You're missing out on all the fun up there!" And this crazy white boy looks at me and says "Why do I need to go up there with those girls when I have you right here". I just looked and smiled "Yeah whatever." Then he said "Ellena, will you give me head?" I was like "Please, that's not my area, the girls are in the hotel." He said "I'll give you $300 if you do," I said hell no, then he said OK will you just jack me off? I just started laughing and said HELL NO! He pulled $500 out of his pocket and said I will give you $500, and all you have to do is jack me off, please, please, please. I still told him NO, then he said OK I will give you $800 to do it, I snatched the money and said OK. It was so funny; his little Peter was so small it didn't even fit in my hand. I think I stroked him about three times and he came. Yeah, I was $800 richer from that. That night I made about $2000 in kickbacks, tips, and extras, so you can see how hard it was not to turn down the money. I was balling out of control.

One morning I was driving home from work and this car pulled up next to me and the cutest little boy was in the car, he asked me to pull over so he could talk to me. I figured why not he was a cutie. We exchanged numbers and came to find out he was 22 years old, at the time I was 30 but I was just going to have fun with him, nothing serious. His name was Gray. He asked if he could take me out and I agreed. We arranged a date and he had me meet him at his apartment. I went inside and there was a grip of guys sitting around. Every last one of them was hitting on me, saying to me "Why you talking to that buster, girl you need to get with me!", so Gray rushed out of the room so he could hurry up and get me out of the lion's den, and we went out and he was a lot of fun. We just went bowling, then for ice cream, and finally to the park and played on the swings.

I agreed to go out with him again, except this time he asked me if I had a friend to bring along as a date for his friend Moe. Tina had long left her husband and had a new baby about the age of Ken's baby, and she was open to dating again, so I invited her to go out with me and Gray and his friend Moe. It was so funny, we walked into the lion's den and of course, there was the usual group of guys sitting around, most of them looking scary except Moe who was kinda cute as he sat playing a video game, keeping his focus on the game until Tina walked in. Tina said "Who's Moe" he looked up and immediately said "Moe here". We learned that there were backup guys to claim to be Moe if Tina was tore up! Moe and Tina clicked instantly, but as the night grew, I realized that Gray was an idiot! Then he ruined the whole night by telling me that he loved me, this was our second date. We were to go out one more time and this time I was going to tell him that things weren't working between us. But that night he came out of the house, I wasn't allowed in the lion's den any longer, and he was high, on sherm! He passed out in the middle of the grass at his apartment, I felt it unnecessary to let him know that we were through. I left and went home!

Meanwhile, back at CLS me and Ant found every chance we could to dip away and have sex in the back of a limo, but Ant was living with some Mexican chick, and the fact that he didn't like kids, or as he claimed he was uncomfortable around them, made it impossible for us to be anything more than what we were. I did like Ant, but it was more of a friendship love, the sex was just convenient. Now I started to realize I had some serious problems because with all the money I was making, I was spending it faster than I made it and I stopped paying my rent. I was evicted from my beautiful home but I moved in with Tina.

She had moved into a house on section 8 and it was a big house so she more than welcomed us. Tina and Moe were getting real close and they went out a lot. He kept trying to hook me up with his friends and I think I went through everyone on his friends list. I went out with another one of his friends Brain, and on the second date, again he told me he loved me! I was so tired of meeting his friends. Then one day he told me that one of his friends needed my expertise on the computer. I was quite the computer whiz and I had impressed Moe a time or two with my skills. His friend CP, ex-drug dealer, was smart with his money and he planned to open a legitimate business. We kept trying to meet up but I was busy working so we kept missing each other. Tina decided that it would be best for Moe to move in with her and for me to move into his apartment which was fine by me because I could have my own space. So me and the kids moved yet again.

One night I had a dream, in the dream I was in New York, I'd never been to New York before, but it felt and looked like New York. I was in a station holding the hands of Symone and Imani and I looked outside and there were two identical large storm clouds in the sky, next to each other. Suddenly they started shooting lightning bolts at each other in a furious rage, and then the clouds turned on the crowd of people on the streets and started hitting the people with the lightning bolts. Everyone started screaming and running all over the place. I saw people on fire falling out in front of me. I started running through the crowd to find my car and when I got through the crowd, Symone and Imani were gone. I stood in the middle of the street screaming and frantically crying out their names while people ran around screaming and crying. Just then I saw the clouds rushing towards me, then with both clouds over my head, I woke up!

My pillow was drenched with sweat and tears, that dream scared me so bad and I knew something was getting ready to happen. A couple of mornings later Symone woke up, she was in kindergarten at the time and she asked me "Mommy remember that time we were homeless and we were just walking around on the streets with nowhere to go?" Me and Alysa looked at each other confused and I assured her that it was just a dream. The next morning Sady called me and told me to turn on the TV, the date September 11, 2001. I thought of my dream as I watched images of the terrorist attack on TV, and all I could think to myself was that I had no job, I knew tourism was getting ready to drop. As I thought of my dream something happened to me mentally, I can't explain it. But it took a toll on my mental health.

At work, my boss, this old white man, was hitting on me hard and it was making me so uncomfortable. One day he called me into his office and he told me that I had a ride that didn't get charged and the total was around $500. I was like "Please"! He told me that either I had to pay it or else. Then he told me to close the door to his office. He looked at my hand and he asked me if I was married. I told him no, he grabbed my hand and said "I know a way you could pay this off." He threw me off guard, my eyes almost welled up with tears, but I didn't want to cry in front of him. I guess he saw my expression and suddenly told me don't worry about it I'll take care of it. That night I was driving on the strip in gridlock traffic and the stress of everything caught up with me and I started having a bad asthma attack. My limo was stuck on Las Vegas Blvd and we were not moving. I called Ken but there was nothing anyone could do because they couldn't get to me. I jumped out of the limo and radioed in to dispatch, I fell out of the limo and someone called 911. When the ambulance got to me, I was at 10% air and I had broken all the blood vessels in my eyes. My boss had been harassing me so much at work that I was falling apart. I know you would think with everything that I've been through, that his little advances should have been nothing, but this is my work environment and there is a level of professionalism that you expect at work and he crossed the line.

The next few weeks it was so dead in Las Vegas, the strip looked like a ghost town, we all knew it was only a matter of days before the layoffs were to begin. Management said it would go by seniority, so do you know how shocked I was when I was laid off and Ant wasn't, I started there months before him. I went to my boss and asked why I was being laid off and this asshole had the nerve to tell me "If you weren't so insubordinate then you would still have your job". I got an attorney and went after CLS for discrimination and sexual harassment. I was smart enough to have a journal with all the dates and times he made advances towards me!

But I went into a deep depression, I couldn't sleep in my bed and I couldn't get up to do anything. Sady tried to kick me out of my depression so we shopped and went to lunch and at night we hung out at the lounges in the casinos. At first, we went out with her family, Mamma, brothers, Tina and Moe, but Sady said she got a wild hair up her ass and she needed to scratch it! Whatever the fuck that meant, but she wanted to go clubbing, so we went clubbing. With me losing my job I couldn't afford the apartment anymore so I moved into a more affordable place, Sady and Ken weren't doing good financially either, so they moved into the same apartments that I moved into.

20. POLTERGEIST HOUSE

After I left CLS Ant and I just lost contact with each other, but finally I met Moe's friend CP. He was more chocolate than I usually like, and that's because my older brother damaged me and made me dislike dark-skinned black men, I know it's sad, and I hate to even say something like that, but he warped my mind as a child. CP had a beautiful smile though, and I am attracted to nice teeth and nice shoes, the shoes tell a lot about a man, and he had on a fresh white pair of K Swiss. He was living with a white girl who was a stripper at Olympic Garden. He asked me if I could come over and help with setting up a website.

CP, although an ex-drug dealer, may not have held any degrees, but he was one smart brotha! He was a penny-pinching business-minded person. I went to his house to help him with the website and as you can imagine, we had sex. From there I was with him almost every day! He and Moe had a business of buying and selling cars from the auction. He also bought houses at auctions so he had a few properties and I had just got approved for Section 8 so he moved me into one of his homes. He was still living with the white girl, but he was back and forth at my house and because he owned the house, he had a key so he came and went as he pleased! We built his website and I helped him formulate paperwork for another business he had. He did hard money loans to people in foreclosure and if they missed one loan payment, their home was quick-deeded over to him. He acquired almost a million dollars' worth of properties doing this. He and ole girl broke up and he moved in with me.

We did all the family stuff; he had a daughter we got on the weekends and we took family trips. We got a boat from a hard money loan and we started going out to Lake Mead on the boat on the weekends. It was fun but me and CP were such opposites except in the bed. Another psycho-sex feign. We had all types of toys, movies, and gadgets. And again, I was recklessly having sex with no protection, and yes you guessed it. I got pregnant! When I told him I was pregnant he instantly told me to get rid of it. Now honestly, I didn't want to have another baby, but I didn't believe in having abortions. But I went to the abortion clinic to inquire.

The first thing they did was give me an ultrasound. The tech showed me the fetus on the screen and the baby was horribly disfigured. She told me it would be in my best interest to abort immediately, so I set up the appointment. Even knowing the fetus was disfigured I felt horrible having an abortion. CP didn't take me, Tina did. After the procedure, I got very sick. I got a stomach infection and I was so sick I couldn't even drink water. CP told me he didn't sign up for this! And I started to notice he was hanging out late and sneaking off to talk on the phone a lot. One of his friends that liked me kept telling me that he had a girlfriend, and I thought he was saying that because he was trying to fuck, but he did in fact have a girlfriend. He told me one night after we had sex and he told me he was moving out, then he cried and told me he loved me but didn't want to be in a relationship with me. When he moved out, I took it hard. I laid on the sofa curled up in a ball, not wanting to do anything.

While CP and I were together, Alysa had a crew of friends that she hung out with from school. One of her friends, Zory hung out a lot at the house. She basically became one of my children. Through odd circumstances, I gained guardianship over her and now legally she was my daughter. It was a little tough taking on a teenager, she was a little feisty and sometimes defiant, but I did what I could to make her feel comfortable. So much so that Alysa thought I was giving Zory better treatment than I was giving her. These were trying times. I was wild myself and here I am trying to raise 2 teenagers. They started sneaking out, and going to parties with their friends! I was getting calls in the middle of the night that a party they were at got shot up and I would have to jump up in the middle of the night to go rescue them! Going out with strange-looking boys with pacifiers and ponytails, having guns pulled on them, car accidents! My head was spinning! Then both of them started working at Burlington and they were robbing Burlington dry. As a parent I should have stopped them, instead, I put in a list of things I needed. SMH!

CP's house I lived in had its own dark energy. By this time, I no longer feared any dark energies. If anything, I became more curious because all my life I had been open to seeing and receiving energy, but nothing I had experienced before would prepare me for what this house had in store for me. The day we moved in someone died about two houses down from us and his body was white bagged almost in front of the house. I didn't think anything of it at first, but I would constantly hear the familiar footsteps in the house. I would be in my bathroom taking a bath and I could feel the presence of someone around me. Then I started having very vivid dreams of killing my older brother, in that house! I would be standing in my room in a pool of blood with blood all over me holding a knife standing over his body and the room is dark but red is pulsating all around me. Then the voices started talking to me in the house. It kept telling me to kill myself, not this again! I had gone several years not hearing the voice but now it had returned! I thought this time for sure I was losing my mind so I decided to see a therapist.

I thought my therapist would be some old white or Asian guy, but he wasn't! He was a fine-ass Egyptian man. And he kept telling me how beautiful and strong and courageous I was, so I wasn't comfortable telling him everything. I didn't want him to think I was crazy. What if he wanted to take me out? My crazy ass! Anyway, I couldn't sleep in my house, so I would sleep 2 hours at a time and wake up in a crazed frenzy. I wouldn't take naps. I was terrified to go to sleep because I kept having sleep paralysis, screaming in my sleep while something had a hold of me, but no sound would come out!

One day, I dropped the kids off at school, I came home and sat on the sofa and before I knew it, I crashed. My energy lifted above my body; I was astro-planning like I did when I was a child. I looked at myself sleeping on the sofa. By now I had learned that if you astro plane your energy can't leave your presence, if it does it's open to other entities taking over it. I started walking away from my body and I started to panic, my energy walked away watching me with a sinister look, and creepily smiled at me as it hit the corner.

I looked around and I was sitting by a pool. The sun was shining and everyone was in white. People were walking by looking at me, and saying something to me but I didn't understand what they were saying. I saw one person pointing with his mouth open with a look of fright on his face, and I turned to see what he was pointing at, but out of nowhere, the beast jumped on my chest. I tried to scream but nothing was coming out. I tried to wake up but it grabbed me by the back of my hair and I could feel its nails digging in my scalp as it held me down. I struggled and cried and just then I remembered to call out to God! I screamed, "GOD PLEASE HELP ME!" And in an instant, my energy returned to my body and the beast let go of my hair and I woke up!

I jumped up and ran out of the house. I was hysterical! This time it physically attacked me! I went back in grabbed my car keys and left. I sat in the car for hours at the girl's school, but I kept feeling the back of my head because it was throbbing. I grabbed a small compact mirror and I tried to look at my scalp, but it was impossible to see. When we got back to the house, I asked Alysa to look at my scalp, but I didn't tell her why. She said did you comb your scalp too hard because you have like these red lines on it. I was shook! After that, I couldn't sleep in that house at all. I was never afraid of my dark energy because it hadn't done anything harmful to me, but this was something different, and it tried to hurt me! I would stay up all night and sleep in the car after I dropped the girls off at school. Then Zory kept claiming to see a midget running around upstairs! She would see and feel the energy in the house. After that, it felt as though the house came alive. I wasn't religious because all my life I've had bad experiences with religious organizations, but I was spiritual! I believe in God, and now I needed Him more than ever before!

When me and CP broke up, I started talking to another one of their friends and he got mad. One day I was at Tina and Moe's house and he walked in. He was on the phone with his new girl talking loudly "No I love you more." Trying to make me jealous, I guess! He told me he wanted to talk to me outside so I went with him. When the door closed, he turned around and grabbed me and told me that I better stop talking to the homeboy, so I got a little smart-ass and said yeah right! He tried to grab me by my neck and I swung to block his arm but accidentally slapped him in the face. He put a key in between his fingers and started swinging on me. He popped me in the head with the key and blood started pouring out of my head! I saw blood and started screaming! Moe ran outside and all he saw was me covered in blood! Tina called the police and Moe started fighting CP! He left.

I hate that the police were called! I hate taking that route. They asked me if I wanted to press charges and I said no. Well, they escalated it to the DA's office, because of his past and now I received a subpoena to go to court and testify against him! I wouldn't go and the courts kept sending me letters saying if I didn't go, I was in contempt of court. So, I went and said he didn't hit me. CP threatened me that if I went to court, he would fuck shit up for me. I was living in his house; he knew everything about me and I just didn't want that headache. After this incident, Moe started watching over me like a hawk. He always made sure I was safe and suggested most nights that me and the kids spend the night at the house with him and Tina. He told me CP beats on women and he wanted me to be safe. Moe became a comforter to me. We started working together, he would give me cars to sell and I would make some cool cash from it. Then he discovered all I could do with a computer.

21. BAKING BREAD

Ken and Sady were going through a divorce. Not only was she a liar, she cheated on my brother, dirty bitch! She would be talking to guys on the phone at the house with Ken sitting right upstairs! Then actual proof of her infidelity surfaced. So, he moved out and we started a business buying and selling computers. We would buy blue screens, replace the motherboard, and load them with pirated Word and Photoshop! I would buy laptops for $50, and resell them for $700! I started making paystubs for people and one day Moe said "What else can you make with Photoshop?" I could make IDs, SS cards, money orders! Then we got a hold of a file that had a rasterized $50 bill on it and we started baking bread! We had crews of people running the loaves all over town, slicing them up, and then bringing us our cut. I had bread everywhere! And because Moe and I started spending so much time together, we started fucking.

Well, that part wasn't my fault. You see I had gone back to school to be a Paralegal after CP and I broke up! I was being super studious, going to class, getting straight A's, and minding my own business. One night Tina called me and asked me to come to the house when I was out of class. I get there, she opens the door and she's wearing some lingerie and drinking something. She asked me if I wanted a drink and I declined. She and Moe sat me down on the couch and she said "Hey, me and Moe was talking and we thought it would be fun to have a threesome. But I was uncomfortable with it so he suggested we do it with someone we know and we both thought of you!" Imagine that! I grabbed a drink and gulped it down because I couldn't believe what she was saying to me.

My better mind told me to get up and walk out the door, but Tina asked me if she could eat me while Moe fucked her from behind. I gulped down another drink (I'm a lightweight). Next thing you know we were in the bedroom and Tina was eating me out while Moe fucked her from behind. It felt weird, yes, I had done this before, but not with someone I was this close to. Then Moe started fucking me and Tina was sucking him and licking me! She wanted me to eat her but I just couldn't, my brain wouldn't let me suck on another woman.

After all was said and done, Tina passed out from being drunk and when Moe thought she was out enough, he rolled over on me and started fucking me, telling me to do it quietly so we don't wake her! So yeah, that's how all that got started, I'm sure he had all this planned out in his mind already. Tina found out that Moe was messing with me on the side and I felt bad because she was my friend! I was still confused as to how we got here. I knew that he orchestrated this whole mess and we both fell for it. But I'm a broken soul so it's easy to get me caught up in mess like this.

Anyway, Tina wanted to fight me, so she came to the house and she knew I would have beat the breaks off her, so she came with her mom and her sister-in-law. I stepped outside like what y'all wanna do, but they didn't want to see me! All three of them against me and they jumped in their car and left.

Moe was always at my house and he had parked a stolen car in my garage and Tina knew this, at the same time Ken and Sady were fighting over custody of their daughter and Ken brought her to the house. Sady called the police and reported a kidnapping and gave the police my address! Luckily that morning we moved the car, but I had bread all over the place loosely hidden. When the police came it was obvious they were looking for a stolen car and a kidnapped child, but they found neither, and thank God they didn't start snooping around. They only didn't because Symone and Imani woke up out of their sleep and walked down the stairs rubbing their eyes with their little nightgowns on! And because I was in Law school, I was learning how to deal with the police!

So, I had a nice conversation with them, non-confrontational, even though they shouldn't have been searching my home without a warrant! The next day I cleaned the whole house out. Sady was mad that we didn't get caught with anything so she called Section 8 and told them Ken was living with me, which he wasn't, he was staying in a hotel but he was using my address, so I got kicked off Section 8. I wanted to kill her! I wanted to catch her off guard and throw a pillowcase over her head, knock her out, and take her to Mt. Charleston. My brother kind of wanted me to, but he thought of his daughter and asked me not to! She doesn't know how he saved her life! I was dead ass serious!

I stopped everything! That was too close. I shut down all operations and I went and got a job. I started working graveyard at the Review-Journal. I was there to sit my ass down and do nothing but work, then entered Big D. He was my supervisor and within a few weeks of me working there, sit my ass down and do nothing, went straight out the window! He asked to take me out. Big D was a thug from Oakland. He was a day sleeper and he drank excessively. But the sex was good! Have I not learned anything??? He had two daughters in Cali with his black ex-wife, another daughter here in Vegas with an Italian woman, and another daughter with an Asian woman, and unknown to me the Asian woman was pregnant with his next daughter.

Things moved way too fast between us, before I knew it, he moved in and I was pregnant! Yup just like that! I wanted a son so bad, but I didn't love Big D, matter of fact after dating him for a while, I realized I barely even liked him. I knew we wouldn't be together long. From the time I found out I was pregnant, I started buying boy clothes. And just like I thought, by the time I was 4 months pregnant we broke up! After moving him into my home, introducing him to my girls, and playing family with this dude. He told me he couldn't be with me because I was too educated and I would demean him, I mean he wasn't lying!

Damany Sekoo II was born August 12th or 13th. Depends on how you look at it. But his birth certificate says the 12th! When I went into labor with Lil D, I was adamant about my son not being born on the 13th. I had a dream while I was pregnant that I had a son who was sitting in a therapist's office talking about killing animals and on the therapist's desk was a calendar that had the 13th on it! When I went into labor on the 12th, I was so serious about him coming into the world on the 12th. Guess what? My doctor was doing a C Section and he got held up in surgery. I went into actual labor at 11 pm. I figured we had enough time to get him out before the stroke of 12! But the nurse comes in at 11:30 and tells me not to push just yet because we're waiting on the doctor.

So, I held back the urge. Right about this time the epidural was wearing off and I'm starting to feel the contractions. The nurse comes in again and says "Almost sweetheart, almost time!" I started panicking because I was stressed and in pain and had an asthma attack. The nurse checked the baby's oxygen level and it was starting to decline! Big D is in the room and he's yelling at the nurse to do something! They put an oxygen mask on me and put an oxygen tube inside for the baby. Now the baby is crowning and I'm screaming in pain and the nurse is still begging me not to push! It's midnight!!! I was crying and Big D got mad and said move I'll deliver him! At 12:15 the freaking doctor finally comes in the room and the minute I saw him I pushed my son out! I waited because I got the feeling the nurses didn't know what to do and I didn't want to chance my son to them!

I WENT THE FUCK OFF!!!! I cussed everyone out in the delivery room! The nurse said "Mom I'll put August 12th at 11:59 PM on his birth record! And that's what she did! So, the 12th it is. Even though he came into the world on the 13th! I'm a little psycho! The following day I was waiting for Big D to come to the hospital, and he didn't show up. That night his apartment got broken into and he was shot in the neck, just inches away from his spine. Geeze! After Big D moved out, we tried to have a relationship, but one night he was drunk and told me he loved me so much and that it was driving him crazy, next thing you know he put a gun to my head and said "If you mess with any other guys, it might make me want to hurt you!" I snapped so fast, even with a gun to my head! I said, "Nigga if you ever put a fucken gun to my head, you better be ready to pull the fucken trigger!" I'm sure that's not the reaction he expected because he put the gun down and cried. I walked out of his apartment and that was it for me. Now I was a single mother of 5! I don't understand the direction of my life, but again, gotta keep pushing!

22. BABY MAKES SIX

I left the Review Journal and I applied for a sales position at a car lot called JD Byrider. I was now into car sales! Just walking in the door, I started selling right away. I met a salesman from a bigger dealership who didn't work with credit as badly as we did, so whenever he couldn't get someone financed, he would bring them straight to me. His volume of sales was legendary, so for me, picking up his bad deals shot my numbers up like crazy! I started selling 15 deals a month, then 20 then 30, almost close to 40! I hit numbers in that dealership that they had never seen before. And of course, my slick ass, if a customer didn't have a paystub or insurance, I would just make it for them to get them rolling!

I was top sales at the dealership, but I can never just relish in my success and happiness. The owner of the dealership was a sexist and racist white man! He literally couldn't stand the fact that a black female was killing numbers at his dealership. He kept hiring white men and told them to get close to me and find out what I was doing and how am I selling so many cars. But the funny thing is the white boys would fake befriend me and then end up liking me as a friend and would tell me what the owner told them to do. I was in a hostile work environment, but I was making so much money, I couldn't leave!

I had left my mom's house in 1998 and it was now 2005. I didn't talk to her for 3 years after I left, and now we barely spoke to each other but one day I wanted to call and talk to my stepdad. I prayed that he would answer the phone and with luck he did! He was mad at me for not staying in touch with him. He told me "Just cuz you mad at your mama don't mean you cut me off!" And I apologized to him. He said, "I'll tell you what, in August bring the kids to the house and they can stay with us for a week!" I said "Even the baby?" And he said "Yep even the baby! Imma go buy him a little crib so he can have somewhere to sleep." I was truly excited! And before we hung up, he told me he loved me, he said I've loved you even before you were born and he laughed. That raised an eyebrow, but nevertheless, I told him I loved him too and got off the phone before Mom could ask to speak to me. He spoke to Alysa and he had arranged to pay her college expenses. She got accepted into Clark Atlanta, so he bought her airline ticket, her luggage and paid some of her tuition cost! That was such a blessing! I didn't know at the time, that would be the last time we spoke to him.

One night Zory came running into my room in a frantic, screaming "There's a man in my room!" I told her she was having a nightmare and to go back to sleep. The next morning, she told me a man was in her room and he crouched down in the corner and gave her a shush motion with his finger. She said he wasn't scary though. Knowing we had so much crazy energy roaming through that house I passed it off as such. A few hours later I got the call that my stepfather passed away that evening in his sleep. Zory cried and said, "It was Grandpa!" And she told me "I think he was looking for you!" Although my biological father had died just a year earlier during Hurricane Katrina, this was the worst death I would ever experience. The year of my dad's death, in 2005 we lost 3 family members, then my stepdad in 2006, and from there, my family lost 3 family members every year around August/September for 4 years, until almost every man in my family was gone! It was very tragic and hard on my family.

JD Byrider was one of the most stressful jobs I ever had! Sure, I was making 6 figures a year, but having a boss who can't stand you because you're black and a woman was too much to bear. He kept hiring men to try to replace me, but I hung in there because I had moved out of CP's crazy poltergeist home and moved into a 3600 square foot beautiful home in a gated community. I had big bills and big responsibilities! I guess when the owner saw that white men weren't working, he decided to bring in the brotha. He hired Davis. I was staying far away from anyone he brought in because he would have me train them and then I would find out their mission. To try to replace me! I had a big corner office; I was at the top of JD Byrider's national leader board and the owner was sick from it. I was receiving big bonuses, dinners to exclusive restaurants, and all types of perks from the company. He hated me but he couldn't fire me because too many people at the top were watching me.

Davis was a goofy-looking dude and he acted just as goofy as he looked. He had a white wife and she was that controlling insecure type. I would barely say Hi to him and he did everything in his power to get me to talk to him. After a few weeks, he came into my office and said "Good morning" I said, "Hey, what's up?" Then he asked me "Did I do something to you?" and I told him "No, why do you ask?" He said, "Because every morning I come in and say hi to you and you barely speak, the Boss told me to train under you and you haven't shown me how to do anything!" He then said "Do you know why I married a white woman??" and I looked up at him as if to say I really don't give a fuck why you married a white woman, but then he said "Because all my life I have loved and been attracted to black women, but they treat me exactly how you're treating me now. They don't talk to me and they turn their nose up at me. The only women that would date me were white girls, so I ended up with a white wife." He said "Anyway I just want you to know how proud I am of you and your accomplishments and I want you to keep winning and pissing him off, lol!", and he walked out of my office. That night when I got home, I kept thinking of what he said to me, and I didn't want to be "that" black girl. My cynical mind said don't train him, but something in my heart said to be the better person, so I went to work the next day and told him I would train him.

He started selling cars and soon we became known as the power duo at JD Byrider. Our work relationship started with him buying me lunch every day, then he asked me if he could take me out to dinner. He told me that he had just finished massage therapist school and that if I ever needed a massage, he had a whole mobile setup. We became friends and he started to tell me how miserable his marriage was, that his wife was psycho, and that he wanted out of the marriage so badly. I just listened. Soon he was texting me "Good morning, Sunshine" every morning, and telling me that I was a breath of fresh air compared to his wife. And then the mistake happened.

He begged me if he could give me a massage and I knew it was a mistake, but it happened anyway. It went from a massage to him kissing all over me to him on top of me! He kept saying "I can't believe I'm with Ellena, I waited so long for this!" He fell in love with me from the moment I let him hit and now he didn't want to be at home anymore, he wanted to be with me 24/7. For as goofy as he looked, he was very freaky! So now here we are in a situationship, and I didn't even know how we got there.

One day he was at home and he called me, he asked if I would stay on the phone with him because his white wife was hitting herself with a weight, to cause bruising, so she could call the police and say that he hit her! I stayed on the phone and had to listen to this bullshit. She hit herself in the head as he was yelling "What are you doing? Stop hitting yourself in the head like that!" Crazy, because if I wasn't on the phone she probably would have had him arrested and he would have had a Domestic Violence case on his hands! Now she couldn't because there was a witness! Eventually, he left his family and moved in and we lived life like a family (my life scenario). He played stepdaddy to the kids, it was only Symone, Imani, and Lil D left at the house. And although he moved in, living in my house, using my electricity, gas, and water, he didn't help me with not one bill! I kept thinking to myself, why am I letting him live here for free? But he kept buying me gifts and taking me and the kids out to expensive restaurants and weekend getaways, so I didn't trip.

Here I was at work one day and I ran to the bathroom and I threw up! I started crying because I knew I was pregnant, and a few weeks later, at work, I had a miscarriage. For someone who was told years ago that I wouldn't be able to get pregnant again after my first child, I sure turned into a fertility garden! 2 miscarriages, 1 aborted fetus, and 3 more babies born! But did I take any preventative action to make sure I didn't get pregnant again? Of course not. The next month I missed my period again! This is too damn fertile, totally ridiculous! Soon I told him, "So since you're living here now, you should be helping me with the bills around here!" He got the nerve to get upset! He said, "I still have to pay the bills where my kids are living and I can't afford to do both!" I asked him "What did you expect? To live here for free?" The next few weeks shit fizzled out real quick, and soon he came and told me "I miss my kids, so I'm going to go home and work things out with my family!" I was like good because I was tired of your ass anyway.

In the midst of our relationship, a few things happened! We both quit JD Byrider, I got into a big fight with the owner and the day I walked out Davis left with me, he had a job lined up for us in Timeshare, at the Grandview. From the gate, he started selling timeshares like crazy, but me, I couldn't sell one to save my life, and the base pay was only $1,000 a week. I could not survive on that type of money, so I was suffering. I didn't tell him about the miscarriage or that I had missed my period, but I had to think long and hard about what I was going to do. The year was 2007 and while selling timeshare the real estate bubble burst! I was laid off from the Grandview because I was low on the totem pole of sales, while Davis retained his position. He moved out, I was now unemployed, with my car note, this big ass house, credit cards, furniture lease payments.

So, I called him and told him that I was pregnant. He told me that wasn't his problem! "Oh really," I thought to myself, "Not your problem, we'll just see about that!" The vindictive side of me came out! He had an old-school Impala with rims that he was renting from Rent-A-Wheel and was late on his payments. So, I called the rim rental spot and told them where to find his car and at what time. While he was at work, they came and took the rims off, and left the car on blocks! He had to leave the car there until he could get it towed, but when he came back for the car, the whole car was gone! Someone stole it! I had absolutely nothing to do with the theft of his car. He thought I had someone steal it, and I told him I knew nothing about his funky ass car.

Again, I called him and asked him what were his thoughts on this pregnancy and he said to get an abortion. I told him I didn't have money for an abortion. I was in financial despair! Everything was crumbling. I was late on my car payment which was now about two months behind. I was running through all my savings and the car was in repo status. So, to get me back, he set me up and my dumb ass fell for the bait! He told me he would pay for the abortion but I had to go to a clinic that he chooses. I went and he wasn't there, but you know who was there? The repo man to get my car while I was inside! His bitch ass had my car repoed while I was inside waiting for him to not show up for an abortion appointment. I guess you play petty games, you get petty prizes. Touche! I wanted him to die. No really, I almost turned gangsta on his ass!

While I was pregnant with his child, this is what he did. I was helpless, I lost my home, my car! I had to pack up everything I owned, put it in storage, and move back to California. I was pregnant, no car, no home, and no money! So, I moved in with my sister and her husband. Oh, depression was on 10 this time! But I'm really a thug! I moved like nothing was bothering me. No tears, no emotions! I just planned to bring another fatherless life into the world

23. CANCER SAVED ME

My sister is not the easiest person to live with but I had to make the best of things. She and her husband were going through some stuff. He was a very abusive, explosive psychopath! Because of my age and me being considered a High-Risk pregnancy, my sister convinced me to go through with the amniocentesis the doctor was recommending. I didn't want to have it done because either way, it didn't make a difference what challenges this pregnancy would have posed, this baby was coming into the world. But I had it done. They took a long thick needle and stuck it right through my stomach and it was the most painful thing ever. They guided the needle through ultrasound to get fluid from around the baby. They make you sign a waiver stating they are not liable if they hurt the baby during the process. Again, I didn't feel good about the procedure but it was done. A few weeks later the doctor's office called me to schedule an appointment to give me the results of the amniocentesis and told me it was urgent.

I went to the appointment, and my doctor, who was an older Asian man sat me down and said, the results of the test came back that the baby was Down Syndrome. I said OK, and he looked at me and asked "What day would you like to schedule the abortion for?" Just nonchalantly. I said "Abortion? I'm 16 weeks!" This man told me "Well because of your situation we can schedule abortions up to 20 weeks, so we have to move fast!" I was in utter shock! First, you just told me my baby has Down syndrome, and now you're suggesting I murder my baby who has a heartbeat and is moving around inside of me! I looked at him and said "I have no intentions of having an abortion" and he said, "You plan to have this baby even though it's going to be severely mentally retarded!" Yes, those were his words! I almost started crying, but I told him "I believe that God makes no mistakes" and he told me "Well if you plan on having this baby, I won't be your doctor" and I told him" I had no intentions of you being my doctor!" I ran out of the office, got to the car, and cried my eyes out!

This was a high-risk pregnancy throughout. I was monitored throughout my whole pregnancy and I went into labor at 27 weeks. I was given Pitocin to stop the contractions, and we held out to 36 weeks. I went into denial about the baby being Downs because she was so active, it almost felt like the baby was doing flips in my stomach, and everything I read said the baby wouldn't be as active as normal pregnancies.

On June 24th Alaia Yasmine almost made her appearance in my sister's car! She crowned in the car and was born within 15 minutes of us arriving at the hospital. She shocked the whole birthing room and I could see the faces of everyone as they looked at her. I couldn't wait to see her. Clearly, she was Down Syndrome, but one of the nurses said out loud, out of her mouth "Someone likes white guys!" I looked at my baby and her skin was as white as this paper, she had blonde hair and blue eyes! It was so quiet you could hear a pin drop! My sister said, "If I hadn't seen her come out of you, I would have thought they switched babies on us!" Davis is the same complexion as me, if not a shade or two darker. I had to think, did I get drunk one night and sleep with the service manager at JD Byrider lol. He was a blonde-haired, blue-eyed white guy that was obsessed with me! I didn't know how, but I was truly confused by her look.

Alaia, although Downs had great muscle tone, she was strong and alert! She latched on instantly and she was growing on regular charts. She was reaching all her milestones and she looked great! My sister and I got into a fight, so I had to move out of her home. We moved into a few weekly's, and life as always was so dysfunctional for me and the kids. We ended up moving in with my older sister. At this point, my children were moving around so much I decided to home-school them. Davis was making about $20 grand a month selling timeshare, so we went to court and his child support was almost $4,000 a month. We moved into an apartment and although that sounds like a good amount of money, Cali is expensive!

The apartment we moved into was in Ontario and it wasn't the best neighborhood. Actually, behind the apartment was a cemetery, and you know my experience with energy, so again we moved into another poltergeist! This time Symone and Imani were old enough to see and experience what I go through! Pictures jumping off the walls, an Egyptian statue I had tried to impale me. And every night out my window there was an alley and, in this alley, a little Hispanic girl was bouncing a ball. I thought I was the only one who heard it until Symone asked me what that noise was she heard every night out the window. I made a joke about it to the property manager and her face turned white as a ghost. She explained to me the little girl drowned in the pool that was now covered in cement and that other people said they would see her walking around at night! The description I gave her fit the girl to a T!

Anyway, somewhere around Alaia's first birthday, she went from being the happiest playful baby to crying all night and appearing to be in pain. She was having high fevers, like 103-105. We would get up in the middle of the night and rush to the ER, but every time we went, they would say, "Oh maybe she's just teething" and they would give her Tylenol and send us home. We started doing this once a week. Her primary care doctor said the same thing! Oh, she looks great mom, give her Tylenol and Gripe water for her tummy ache. I switched doctors, just to see if I could get a second opinion, and that doctor literally said the same thing!

Alaia went from standing up and almost walking to being so weak she could hardly get on her knees to crawl. Then she went to not even being able to lift her head in a matter of 3 months. I had to pull out her Boppy pillow because she started sleeping so much. From the time she was 3 months old, she had been receiving services from Inland Regional Services and her therapist took note of her declining health. My mom looked at Alaia one Labor Day and she told me "You need to find out what's going on with her, she doesn't look well!" I told her that we had been back and forth to the ER and 2 different doctors, and she said "Well, go see a third doctor." So, we did. I made an appointment with another doctor, and just like the last two, she whizzed into the room, looked her over, and said, "She looks good." Then she said, "Just give her some Tylenol and some gripe water!" Those instructions started to infuriate me!

One day her therapist told me Alaia's progress was declining, so I told her what we had been going through for the last 6 months. She gave me a number to a doctor that deals specifically with special needs children, so I thought, here we go again! Doctor number 4. November 3rd, 2009, I left the other kids with my older sis while I took Alaia to the doctor. We got there about 3 pm. The office was busy and the doctor was bouncing around from room to room, just like all the other doctors. She walks in and Alaia had a slight fever that day. She felt her stomach and said "Her tummy is distended" I didn't know what that meant. She has a touch of albinism. She also said "She doesn't look full Downs, maybe Mosaic" Then she said, "She has a slight fever, we'll give her some Tylenol and some Gripe water for her tummy!" When I tell you, those words made me lose it! I broke out in tears and I told the doctor "You need to sit down and listen to me! For 6 months every doctor keeps saying the same thing! Tylenol and Gripe water! My baby is very sick and I don't know what's wrong with her, she's having high fevers, she cries uncontrollably, she's weak, her skin looks greyish, she has dark circles around her eyes, she appears to be in pain and I don't know what to do! You're the fourth doctor to tell me the same thing and I need a better answer!" And for the first time, a doctor stopped and looked at me and she asked me "Has she had any blood work done?" And I told her NO! Out of the four doctors we have seen, this is the first time anyone asked me that. The doctor ordered a finger prick, and within a few minutes a nurse came in and said the doctor ordered a stat full CBC.

It was now close to 5 o'clock and we had been in the office for over two hours. The waiting room was cleared out and finally, the doctor came back in the room. She told me "Mom, I need you to take your baby straight to Loma Linda Hospital. There is a full team waiting for you when you get there. Please don't go home, go straight to the hospital. Your baby is severely anemic and could possibly have cancer." From there all I heard was blah blah blah blah blah blah! I was so nervous I was shaking. I hurried to the car, buckled her in her seat and we hit the freeway! It was 5:00 pm and the traffic was horrendous! I called my older sis and she didn't answer. I called my other sister; she's a Respiratory Therapist and I knew she would be calm. I was in tears telling her we were heading to Loma Linda and that Alaia may have cancer.

When we got there, I went to the counter and gave our names and within minutes, doctors, nurses, phlebotomists, the whole crew came out! I was pulled to one side to check her in while she was being triaged. They told me "Mom things are going to move really fast right now but your baby's blood count is fatally low and we're going to have to give her an emergency blood transfusion!" WHAT? I always heard negative things about blood transfusions, and they were rushing me to sign the papers. There was so much going on, and I didn't realize from the time I took her out of the car and got her inside she was nonresponsive. She was hooked up to so much stuff so fast I felt like I couldn't breathe. Then a nurse saw my face and my confusion and she slowed everything down for me. She sat me down and explained the procedure Alaia needed, she reassured me the blood they give the babies is triple-screened and that it will help her. So, I signed the papers and within minutes a bag of blood was being pumped into my baby's tiny frail arm. The first bag wasn't enough. I had to sign for another bag. Her heart rate started to improve but she still needed one more bag! It was now 4 am and the third bag was midway when Alaia opened her eyes and looked around as if to say "What the heck is going on here?" but she did something she hadn't done in months, she sat up and smiled! A tear of relief rolled down my cheek.

The nurse told me that Alaia was scheduled to have a bone marrow biopsy at 9:30 that morning, the nurse told me the procedure would take about 30 minutes but she would have to be sedated with propofol. The first time I ever heard the word Propofol was at the death of Michael Jackson, a day after Alaia's first birthday, so you know that didn't sit well with me. It was overwhelmingly heartbreaking to see my baby sedated with this powerful drug. Once she was out, I was pushed out of the room while a team of doctors went to work on her. I went numb! The nurses told me that we would be in the hospital indefinitely (what does that mean?), what about the other kids, what about my home?

After Alaia's procedure she would be out for a bit so while I had my sister there, I took advantage of the time to go home and pack a few items for our indefinite hospital stay. The kids were with my older sis which was fine because I wasn't prepared to lay such a heavy burden on them just yet. I ran home showered, grabbed some clothes and toiletries for me and Laia and it was back to the hospital. When I got back to the room my sister was sitting in a daze, she told me that the doctor had come in looking for me while I was gone. Alaia has Leukemia and we're scheduled to have a meeting with the doctors and meet our team at 6:30 pm. Leukemia, I'm going to be totally honest, I didn't even know that black people got Leukemia. I barely even knew what it was, besides our family doesn't get stuff like this! Our babies don't get cancer or any other terminal illnesses! Alaia came out of her drugged sleep very groggy and fussy and she didn't want to eat anything, oh yeah eat, I hadn't done that since yesterday but I had absolutely no appetite at all.

Our nurse came in to watch Alaia as me and my sister went to a round table forum to meet the Doctors and a host of other nurses and staff. They put an enormous amount of papers in front of me explaining A.L.L. Acute Lymphoblastic Leukemia. Cancer of the bone marrow, and the best explanation they could give me as to why my baby has this disease is that Cancer cells just explode themselves into existence! That's it! No pre-existing conditions, not necessarily hereditary but common in children with Down Syndrome. While I was pregnant with Alaia the genetics specialist sent me all types of information on what to expect with children with Downs- congenital heart defects, she had a small hole in her heart at birth that closed on its own by the time she was four months. Intestinal blockage, no problem with that, then I remembered Leukemia- common among children with Down Syndrome but I never even thought twice about the possibility of that happening. They talked I listened, and a lot of it was very confusing to me, I have an Associate's degree in Paralegal Studies so I know legal jargon, but not medical and they talked to me as if I was a medical expert. But as they went along, they kept informing me that everything they were saying to me was in the paperwork.

Decision time again, I was asked if I wanted Alaia to participate in clinical studies as a way to find better treatments for the future of Blood

Cancers, heck I don't know, sure why not. Then after an hour of Leukemia 101, her doctor asked me if I had any questions. I couldn't ask questions at that time because I needed all the information to marinate in my head and I needed to go back and read the information so I could have a clear understanding of everything that was just said to me. He looked at me and said "Miss Smith, it's ok to cry, you can break down, we understand" but I couldn't cry. In the last 24 hours, I found out that my baby has cancer, she needed 3 emergency blood transfusions, we didn't sleep or eat, she had a bone marrow biopsy, and she was drugged with propofol. I learned that we would be in the hospital indefinitely, my children were misplaced, the groceries I just bought were going to go bad, and how are the bills going to get paid. You just gave me a boatload of information on Leukemia, something I knew nothing about until 2 hours ago and you expect a response from me, I've got nothing. He tells me that she will begin chemotherapy immediately.

The next morning Alaia's IV was removed and she received what was supposed to be a more permanent line called a PICC line, it would be her portal for blood draws and chemotherapy so she didn't have to be poked for the many procedures that she would soon be facing. That same morning, she also had a Lumbar Puncture which is a needle in her spine to draw fluid from her brain to make sure that the cancer isn't spreading to her spine and also samples for clinical testing and to give her Intrathecal Methotrexate, which was her chemo medicine. I figured we had been here two days, I guess it was time to tell the other children what was going on with their sister, I had asked my family not to tell them and to let me talk to them about it. It was so crazy; it had been only two days but it felt as if I hadn't seen them in months.

Because of the different viruses that were going around, Swine flu, and H1N1, the children were strictly forbidden to come see the baby. My sis brought them to the hospital lobby and she stayed with Alaia while I took them out. Lil D had just turned 4, and when he saw me, he ran to me and grabbed my legs and from that moment he wouldn't let them go. We went to Del Taco, I felt I should finally eat something and take advantage of being able to actually get some food, the hospital doesn't feed the parents, you're on your own with that one, even though I can't leave my baby alone per hospital rules. My children are very smart, I knew that no one told them anything but they responded as if they already knew. I could tell they were shocked but wanted to be strong and right now I didn't want them to be strong because I felt they would break down when I wasn't there to console them and someone else would have to do it for me.

They were very sad and solemn; Symone 13 and Imani 11 were already being home-schooled so there would be no interruptions there. We have become a very close family because regardless of everything we have gone through, my kids remained right by my side! I'm very particular about what they are exposed to, what they see, hear, eat, and learn. This separation was going to be tough. When we got back to the hospital and it was time for our goodbyes, in the lobby Lil D wrapped himself around my legs and screamed at the top of his lungs while his sisters tried prying him off me. I cried like a baby, it was one of the hardest days of my life....I dragged myself back to the room and Alaia was up eating, smiling, laughing and it was the exact thing I needed to see at that moment.

After a few nights of hospital life Alaia slept through the night! We hadn't had much sleep since being there, she's so used to sleeping with me. She has had two more blood transfusions and it is really helping her, she's eating, playing with toys, and being her old silly self again! I had wished the kids could see her like this. She started on a new round of chemo drugs, Mercaptopurine, Methotrexate, and Diflucan. She had to take pills and she took them like a champ, her nurses were so impressed, that they told me the older kids fight to take them. I started to develop cabin fever. It took me a couple of days to figure out the shower appointment thing. This big floor of parents and there is only one shower for all of us to share and if you miss your shower appointment, tough luck. Parents can't use the bathroom in the room, for patient use only so I have to go out of the room to use it and arrange for a nurse to keep an eye on Alaia for me while I'm out of the room, so I've developed a trucker's bladder. Good thing I worked as a limo driver and had already learned that skill. It's even a feat to get out to brush my teeth, this felt like being in jail all over again! Symone was blowing my phone up all the time, she called me, texted me, and stayed hitting me on

Facebook, I know she missed me terribly and I missed them like crazy.

We stayed in the hospital for 45 days! Alaia was released and then hospitalized again and again. For the next year, we spent 282 days out of 365 in the hospital! Fevers, infections, low weight! It was a whirlwind year. I talked to parents whose children were dying and there was nothing they could do except make their child comfortable until their last day. It was very emotional and very frustrating because Alaia was not getting better, on the contrary, she was getting worse! She was constantly vomiting and having diarrhea and it was affecting her weight. She dropped down to a scary 14 pounds, she looked like skin and bones. She had to have a feeding tube inserted and we had to carry her feeding tube with us everywhere we went. Some days Alaia had to go NPO, which meant she was going to have a procedure and she couldn't have anything by mouth, no food no water. When she went NPO I did it with her.

I started reading the Bible again. In jail I read it all the way through, but this time I read it with so much clarity. It sent me on a Spiritual journey that I can't explain. But what I can say, is that when you start to open your eyes to the real God, dark spirits will attack! And I had to learn what that looked like! In this year of dealing with all of Alaia's health issues, we lost our apartment, which was the most stability I had since moving back to Cali. But this had become so common in my life it no longer bothered me. I had no choice but to move in with my mom. But guess what? She put us out! Because she said Lil D was too much for her. Yes, her grandson was too much for her! Of course, he was loud and active! He's 5!!! With nowhere for us to go, me and my children slept in my car next door to my mom's house. With a child who has cancer. I was in disbelief! During the time we were back and forth in the hospital, Davis was fighting me in court over his child support, so the amount kept fluctuating.

24. THE BATTLE

Thankfully I was on this Spiritual journey because it allowed me to laugh and smile through it all. I was now in a constant Spiritual battle! I wanted and needed clarity and answers. Because I grew up in the church, I always thought it was a sin to go to Tarot readers or Palm Readers, but in life, I wasn't getting any answers, so I decided to go to a Palm Reader. I nervously entered through the front door, standing and looking around. An Indian woman was sitting inside, and I hadn't even said Hi to her when she said "You have a very dark energy that surrounds you. It's not from you or your mother, or your mother's mother! As a matter of fact, it's not necessarily from your mother's side. But this energy, shall we call it Tracy (remember my imaginary friend as a child was named Tracy) is enraged! Because you want to break free from it and that's not what it has planned. You, right now are experiencing a life tragedy, but you have to remember, that when you have tragedy in your life you allow your dark energy to grow strength! You have to be strong and defeat it this time! You will gain the strength you need from those closest to you!"

Y'ALL! I hadn't said ONE WORD YET! I broke down in tears! She sat me down and said "You're on an educational journey, continue on that path, it will be your redeeming victory in the end! Remember, even though it's been hard, it's going to get HARDER before it gets BETTER! But the Spiritual path that you are on is the correct path. Don't look to the left, don't look to the right! Keep your focus straight ahead, even when spirits rage, don't be scared don't stray from your path, or you will continue to do this over and over again! That'll be $50!" I cheerfully paid her! I couldn't believe what I had just heard come out of this woman's mouth! This was a turning point for me. It changed my heart and my relationship with my children. They felt our financial woes, but I connected them to nature during this time and taught them how to be grateful! After a little over a week of sleeping in the car, I was able to get us into a weekly. Then after a few months of being in the weekly, Tray's little sister, Shanna offered for me and the kids to come stay at her home.

Sadly and suddenly Tray's mom had passed away and her dad moved to Atlanta, so Shanna was living in the house alone. So yes, I was excited to move the children into a house. Of course, I couldn't work with all of this going on, so I started baking from the house and Tastee Treatz was born! Me and Symone had an incredible bonding moment. We would wake up at the crack of dawn, and if I wasn't up, she got me up. We baked desserts; Banana Pudding, German Chocolate Cake, Red Velvet Cake, Sock it to me Cake, Sweet Potato Cookies, and Peach Cobbler! We also made stuffed Focaccia bread, these were items I invented, like the Sweet Potato Cookies and the Focaccia. I made mini versions of the classic desserts I grew up with. All homemade, from scratch, with natural fresh ingredients. By noon we would hit all the local Beauty salons and Barber shops, pretty much selling out every time we went out!

But just as the Palm Reader had told me, a spiritual battle was brewing! Something that would be intense, but her words prepared me for what was to come! I know now that energy follows me and I am able to see energy. I had no fear of the energy that was in Shanna's home because it was very familiar. It started with my dreams again. I would hear footsteps and the walls breathing very heavily at night, and it would wake me out of my sleep. In my room, there were mirrors all around and I would wake up out of sleep and see a light moving around in the kitchen. Tray's mom had a business of baking out of her home. So, I knew it was her just in her kitchen, as she always was when I would come to the house.

She made the best Red Velvet Cake and Chocolate Chip cookies that touched this planet! She was the inspiration behind Tastee Treatz, but I felt her energy in the kitchen, even when I cooked in it! I have always been afraid to take naps and it's something I just wouldn't do, but one day I was exhausted and I laid on the sofa and fell asleep. Some of this I remembered, some I don't, it was just what my daughter Alysa told me I did. I was sleeping and Alysa, who was at college nearby, at Cal Baptist University in Riverside, knocked on the door. She told me I opened the door with my eyes closed. I told her to sit down and I pulled out a piece of paper and a pen. I started writing fast like shorthand, with my eyes closed. When I awakened, I looked over and saw her sitting there. I was in a cloud of confusion, and when I looked down at the paper I had been writing on, there was a series of letters and numbers. I had no idea of what had just happened to me, but Alysa said "Mommy it was like you were possessed!"

I started to study what I had written. I pulled out my laptop and became obsessed with decoding whatever message was on that paper. I fell down the Rabbit Hole! I wrote in Gematria, a term I had never heard of before in my life. I started to decode my name, my birthdate, my blood type, and then online I found the MK Ultra playbook! I became so engulfed in the Illuminate you would have thought I was trying to join. But it brought so much sense to my life! Rather you believe it or not, or if you think people are conspiracy theorists or not, this Rabbit Hole helped me make sense of my life!

In the MK Ultra playbook, part of mind control is having victims who have been abused sexually at a very young age. Having them exposed to abuse and neglect. Coming from homes that are improvised, witnessing violence, drug or alcohol abuse! Techniques used by the government to download images into the minds of these people so they can use them for their benefit! Then I started to look at the lives of celebrities, realizing that most celebrities have a backstory of abuse! It all made sense to me. Understanding that maybe I wasn't crazy and that I wasn't alone!

A series of unexplained events took place in the house. I have always heard a high-pitched ringing noise randomly in my ear all my life, but now the kids were asking me "What's that ringing noise I'm hearing?" Then things would randomly jump off counters onto the floor, like a gallon of milk! Or a glass! Toys got tossed across the room! Alaia would sit up in the middle of the night and point in the corner screaming! One day my body vibrated so hard, that I lifted off the bed and nearly fell to the ground when

I looked at myself in the mirror! I didn't know how to explain to the kids what was happening and they were terrified! But moving didn't make a difference because whatever I had within me would be with us wherever we moved to. Alaia was so focused on this energy, to where she no longer feared it and was conversing with it.

This is a story just to give insight as to what we were experiencing. The TV remote came up missing. We searched the house high and low for that dang remote! It was nowhere to be found. We moved the sofa, emptied drawers, looked in between cushions, planters. You name it! We looked there. It was now a week later and still no remote. We're sitting in the den watching TV and there was a crash in the living room. Me, Shanna, and the older kids get up to see what happened. Alaia was still very weak and still not standing on her own. We noticed that a vase in the living room fell over and broke. Shanna went to clean it up and I went back to the den because we had left Alaia. When I got to the den Alaia was standing up holding onto the coffee table looking up to the corner of the room babbling! Next to her hand was the remote!!! She didn't see me come into the den, but I approached her very slowly because my mouth was wide open, my hand was over my mouth, and my eyes were bucked out of their sockets! The kids came running into the den and when they came Symone yelled "Oh My God!" and Alaia fell to the ground on her butt! And she looked at me and laughed! Now I know most of you would say throw the whole baby away! Lol But I came to terms with the energy that moved amongst us, and realized that fear was the very thing that fueled it!

25. THE REDEMPTION

I had a sense of relief, as crazy as that may sound! Knowing that others saw what I had seen my whole life. I just wanted to focus on Alaia's health and get her better. One morning I woke up and Alaia's whole eye was swollen! I rushed her to Loma Linda. They instantly put us into Isolation. She had a fever and they stated she had an infection that could possibly spread to other parts of her body, including her organs. I knew we would be here for a while. They started an anti-viral on her and because we were in Isolation I couldn't leave the room and we couldn't have any visitors. After 7 days I noticed she was getting better and the swelling was almost gone. But they kept us in Isolation for a few more days as a precautionary.

After 10 days we were moved to a regular room, where we sat and waited for her doctor to come talk to us. I didn't see her doctor for a week!!! So now we've been here for over two weeks. Finally, her doctor comes in and looks at her eye. He said there's still some redness and swelling so he wants to keep her under observation! It is now almost 30 days since we've been here! She only had some puffiness left in her eye and the doctor came in and said he wanted to do a probe on her eye. But we had a specialist come in and tell us that she did not have an active infection. Her doctor tells me he's going to take her just to look closer at it. They come back after an hour or so and Alaia has a patch on her eye! This doctor cut into my baby's eye! Even after he was told there was not an active infection!

I LOST IT! I told her doctor "THIS IS MY CHILD! NOT YOUR BILLABLE HOUR OR YOUR PAYCHECK!" I WAS LIVID! I called Alysa to come get us! I pulled out every IV, every tube attached. The nurses were screaming at me "WHAT ARE YOU DOING?" I told them "We're leaving!" A nurse said, "No Miss Smith you can't do this!" A nurse tried to stand in the way of the door and I picked up a chair! They tried to call her doctor and his punk ass wouldn't come after I cussed his ass out! Then they put a paper in my face saying "You have to sign this form saying you're taking her without doctors' consent!" I ripped it up and threw it in the nurse's face! I gave Alaia to Alysa, grabbed our stuff and we left Loma Linda!

After this, I started to pay attention to everything now. The back and forth to the hospital, the medications she was on, the weight loss. I had enough, and I asked myself "Is there a natural way to cure cancer?" I grabbed my laptop and typed that into my Google search bar. The first thing that popped up was "Dr. Sebi cures cancer in Mexico!" I clicked the link and I read a little of the court documents on file, then I read his story. Next, a link to his full protocol popped up! "The exact method I use to cure cancer, by Dr. Sebi!" I read the whole thing in less than an hour! It stated that it's best if the patient hasn't started chemo yet, but if they have, take them off the chemo immediately! I stared into space and my mind went all over the place! Take her off chemo? What if that makes her sicker? What if she dies? This is terrifying! I've trusted the doctors all this time! But look at her! She looks like she's dying! I was on a literal emotional rollercoaster! After a few days of more research, I just said "God, please guide me in the right direction to heal my child!" And the next thing I heard was "STOP GIVING HER THE CHEMO!"

There it was! My mind was made. Now the first part of the protocol was to fast for 15-30 days on just grape juice, from grapes with seeds. Seeing that we lived in Rancho Cucamonga, where the whole town was rows and rows of grape fields, the kids and I got up early and went to the vineyards and started picking grapes! The Mexican field workers looked over at us in confusion, but they didn't stop us. Then it said to give the patient 2 tablespoons of Irish sea moss daily. Where the heck do I find that? I went to the only place I thought would have it. Simply Wholesome in LA. When I went in and asked for sea moss, the guy working on the vitamin side stared at me for a minute, and he said "What do you need it for?" I explained Alaia's situation and then he took me almost to the back of the store and he showed me the different sea moss!

He told me that the best water to give her is oxygen water with a drop of colloidal silver in it. I thought, ok it won't hurt. And lastly part of the protocol was the detox bath. 1 cup of sea salt, 1 cup of baking soda, and a few drops of eucalyptus oil. At the time Alaia was not taking anything by mouth, not even water! I took a syringe and I filled it with grape juice and squeezed it into her mouth. At first, she spit it out, but then she started to get the taste of it and smacked her lips. I had talked to the older kids with cancer in the hospital and they told me when they're on chemo they have a metallic taste in their mouth and it makes their food taste funny. But I could tell she got the full flavor of the juice! I pushed more in and she swallowed it! Each day I started to slowly decrease her dosage of her chemo meds! Alaia, within a week, was drinking a full liter of grape juice and I was able to lower the amount of nutrition she was receiving from the feeding tube! Now she was drinking the grape juice and water by mouth! I gave her the detox bath and my God! The water turned black! After 15 days I started giving her fruit smoothies and she was tearing them up. Within 30 days, her strength came back. Her color came back. She started crawling again! I stopped giving her the home chemo, but we still had to go to clinic once a month and I didn't even want to do that, but we went.

Each time we go to clinic, her doctor tests her blood levels, and as you can guess, her doctor comes in the room with a strange look on his face. This was our first time seeing his punk ass since being in Loma Linda and I really didn't have a lot of words for him. He rolled his seat up close to me and said "What are you doing with her?" I looked at him and asked, "What do you mean?" He said "Are you still giving her the chemo? Because going against doctor's order can be frowned upon by law!" He peered at me. I told him "Yes I'm still giving her chemo!" Then he said, "Her blood count is better than a healthy adult!" I said, "That's good news, correct?" And peered back at him!

After that, we missed the next appointment and I got a call from the clinic stating that we had to reschedule, so I pushed it back a little and we went in. It was now just about 3 months since I started Dr. Sebi's protocol. The day I scheduled for clinic her regular doctor wasn't there. The doctor on duty that day came in and said, "Your daughter's blood counts are reading normal. I don't think she needs to do a treatment today! Why don't you follow up with your doctor at another date." I was ecstatic! I pushed as far as I could to schedule her next appointment. When we got there, she did her blood draw and her doctor came in and told me that Alaia was in Remission! Usually, when cancer patients go into remission it's a big deal! All the nurses come out, they clap and the child gets to ring the bell! None of that for us! The doctor told me "It's parents like you that cause their children to relapse. We'll see you back!"

26. THE CALM AFTER THE STORMS

I had moved out of Shanna's house and then got an apartment with my older sis. That didn't work so we moved again into the home of a friend of a friend. Again, we moved into a home where tragically my friend's mother and sister were killed in a horrible automobile accident and their energy was all over the house. In this house, my energy was very vulnerable. I was having the craziest dreams, where celebrities were talking to me, having conversations with me. Taking me on tours of their homes, but then I realized why! My energy was being summoned by elites.

Let me explain what I have learned. If you know anything about the MK Ultra playbook you learn that certain energies can be called upon and used for certain purposes, hence the reason why I spent most of my life locked up in a chamber as a child. I've heard everyone call me crazy, a conspiracy theorist, and everything in between, but I know there is someone out there who has shared my experiences. My children were terrified of what they saw and experienced in that house, so much so that they refuse to speak of it to this day. They will confirm, but they don't like having conversations about it.

I enrolled in school with Liberty University Pre-Law program, to occupy my mind and I signed the kids up with Kids Management to do background work in Hollywood! We're always all over the place. I'm just a hustler and I need to constantly be moving. Alaia was pretty much done with treatment other than the doctor told us to keep up with clinic for the next few months, but at this point, I was over it!

The first time we missed clinic we got a call from the office. I was told again that it was against my contractual agreement to miss any of Alaia's appointments! Then I got a call that child welfare services wanted to meet with us. THEN I got a call from a completely different number. I spoke to a woman who told me that I signed an agreement to donate Alaia's cerebrum fluid for cancer research, and if I didn't bring her in for a spinal tap I would be in violation of our agreement, a court order could be issued to obtain her spinal fluid and I would be subjected to investigation from child protective services! Honestly, I was scared.

Loma Linda was blowing my phone up! Leaving me messages and asking for my current mailing address. I felt like it was only a matter of time before they got my address and because I was so unstable, I felt as if they could send CPS in on me and take all my children. My best bet was to move back to Vegas. We packed up our stuff and left California. We left everything behind, Tastee Treatz and Lil D was getting Director picked for roles in TV shows and movies. Symone and Imani both were working on shows. But I wasn't taking any chances. And honestly being back in the Hollywood realm, this time with my eyes wide open, I realized I didn't want my children anywhere near that life!

So, we went incognito. I didn't want to have an address for a while so we stayed again in weeklies. But one problem! Alaia still had her porta Cath in her and I knew I would have to go get it removed. I let a few months pass, then I called to schedule her outpatient surgery to have it removed.

I was terrified taking her to the surgery center that day, but God was with us! Her doctor wasn't there, the surgery went quick and smooth, and her recovery time was 1 hour and then she was released to me! We left, I grabbed the other kids and immediately hit the road right back to Las Vegas!

27. CONCLUSION

Over the last 13 years, Alaia has remained cancer-free! 13 years in remission! During the time that I've been back in Las Vegas, I sold cars and opened a business. I opened the FIRST and only, black-owned and women-owned Drive Thru mini mart in Las Vegas! The store allowed small black-owned businesses the opportunity to have their products on the shelf of an actual brick-and-mortar store! At one time we had over 50 businesses on the shelves of our store! The store connected me to the community in such a way, that caused changes in me and my direction in life. And it was made very clear to me what that direction was to be.

When I opened the store, I was moving so fast that I didn't look at Alaia. Being on the move meant our diet went downhill. We ate chicken sandwiches, fries, tacos, and burritos daily. Alaia was gaining weight and to keep her from being bored I gave her snacks. On May 22, 2022, Alaia passed out on our bathroom floor! When the paramedics came her Blood Glucose level was 800!!! She went into a 3-day coma. I spent those 3 days in deep meditation as I lay by her side! On the third day when she opened her eyes, I knew what my mission was to be! I was going to become a Health and Nutrition Coach and I was going to get her Glucose back to normal!

We stayed in the ICU for 2 weeks! The minute she was released from the hospital WE went on a 30-day fast! In 30 days, her Blood Glucose went from 800 to 135, then within the next 2 months it went to 90! All through changing her diet. The day Alaia went to the hospital she weighed 226 pounds on her little 4'8 frame. Within 6 months she weighed 135 pounds! A weight loss of a whopping 91 pounds!!!

I realized that I need to share what I know with others. I needed to share with people that First: It doesn't matter what you go through in life, with GOD you can overcome all things and come out victorious! Second: That any disease in the body can be healed by fasting and eating the right foods. Third: Love is the highest form of vibration and it can release anyone from the bondage of depression. So, trust GOD eat good FOOD, and LOVE hard! These are the keys to Happiness and longevity in Life!

My life has been tragically tumultuous! From my father's abuse of our family to being raised in a racist community. A 5-year-old child that was sexually assaulted, was almost raped. Blackmailed by my own brother and endured molestation and abuse on an almost daily basis. Abusive punishment and neglect from my mother. Learning to be a thief at a young age. Being highly promiscuous, then sexually active as a young girl. Raped, used by men, criminalization, incarceration, homelessness, single parenting, fighting, violence, loss of multiple pregnancies, depression, suicidal, attacked by dark energies, and then my baby fighting terminal illnesses! UNREAL! There were definitely times that I didn't want to go on.

Life is so heavy and trying to navigate through all this has been overwhelming and exhausting! But I learned that everything happens for a reason! You don't see it at the time of your experience, all you see is the trauma and the pain. But when God has a special covering over your head, you make it out and one day you get to look back and say, I see why all this happened! I know that God exists through me! And every earthly experience I endure is God having a human experience! All energies are connected and learning this is the biggest lesson we can accomplish while we are here!

Every day is still a struggle for me, but I get up and keep moving! Healing is a life-long journey!   And I'm just here for the ride!

ABOUT THE AUTHOR

Ellena Smith,

A 54-year-old Entrepreneur, Life Health and Nutrition Coach, and Life Insurance Agent living in Las Vegas for the past 23 years, originally from Southern California.

Ellena was born in Inglewood CA, and lived in Watts until 2. Then her family moved to the suburbs of Southern California. She was the victim of trauma from an early age, being sexually assaulted and molested at the age of 5. Because of her parent's long work hours, she and her siblings were forced to raise themselves which started her to a life of crime at an early age. Because of her early trauma, Ellena lived a life of promiscuity and crime from selling her body to getting involved in forgery, check fraud, and credit card fraud. She was arrested in LA and Kansas City and released on an OR but that didn't end her criminal activities. Ultimately, she was arrested in Norwalk CA on Fraud charges where she spent over a year in Sybil Brand jail for women and then sent to Chowchilla State Prison.

After her release, Ellena went to school, first for cosmetology and business, and assisted with the opening of Shear Joy Beauty Salon in LA, CA. After that, she went to school for Paralegal studies and then studied Pre-Law at Liberty University. Ellena has had several business ventures, such as Tastee Treatz by Layne Bake Shop. She also worked in car sales for 20 years. In 2020 she opened Easy Days Drive Thru Mini Mart in Las Vegas, NV. After closing the business due to the COVID pandemic, she got certified as a Life Coach and a Diet, Health & Nutrition Coach and studied Herbalism! Ellena is using her past trauma to help others who may be dealing with these issues rewrite their life story, so they can stop looking in the rearview mirror of the past and look out the front windshield to a better tomorrow!

Made in the USA
Columbia, SC
22 November 2024

47198332R00087